Report of the secretary of the Treasury to the House of Representatives, relative to a provision for the support of the public credit of the United States, in conformity to a resolution of the twenty-first day of September

Gale ECCO Print Editions

Relive history with *Eighteenth Century Collections Online*, now available in print for the independent historian and collector. This series includes the most significant English-language and foreign-language works printed in Great Britain during the eighteenth century, and is organized in seven different subject areas including literature and language; medicine, science, and technology; and religion and philosophy. The collection also includes thousands of important works from the Americas.

The eighteenth century has been called "The Age of Enlightenment." It was a period of rapid advance in print culture and publishing, in world exploration, and in the rapid growth of science and technology – all of which had a profound impact on the political and cultural landscape. At the end of the century the American Revolution, French Revolution and Industrial Revolution, perhaps three of the most significant events in modern history, set in motion developments that eventually dominated world political, economic, and social life.

In a groundbreaking effort, Gale initiated a revolution of its own: digitization of epic proportions to preserve these invaluable works in the largest online archive of its kind. Contributions from major world libraries constitute over 175,000 original printed works. Scanned images of the actual pages, rather than transcriptions, recreate the works *as they first appeared.*

Now for the first time, these high-quality digital scans of original works are available via print-on-demand, making them readily accessible to libraries, students, independent scholars, and readers of all ages.

For our initial release we have created seven robust collections to form one the world's most comprehensive catalogs of 18th century works.

Initial Gale ECCO Print Editions collections include:

History and Geography
Rich in titles on English life and social history, this collection spans the world as it was known to eighteenth-century historians and explorers. Titles include a wealth of travel accounts and diaries, histories of nations from throughout the world, and maps and charts of a world that was still being discovered. Students of the War of American Independence will find fascinating accounts from the British side of conflict.

Social Science

Delve into what it was like to live during the eighteenth century by reading the first-hand accounts of everyday people, including city dwellers and farmers, businessmen and bankers, artisans and merchants, artists and their patrons, politicians and their constituents. Original texts make the American, French, and Industrial revolutions vividly contemporary.

Medicine, Science and Technology

Medical theory and practice of the 1700s developed rapidly, as is evidenced by the extensive collection, which includes descriptions of diseases, their conditions, and treatments. Books on science and technology, agriculture, military technology, natural philosophy, even cookbooks, are all contained here.

Literature and Language

Western literary study flows out of eighteenth-century works by Alexander Pope, Daniel Defoe, Henry Fielding, Frances Burney, Denis Diderot, Johann Gottfried Herder, Johann Wolfgang von Goethe, and others. Experience the birth of the modern novel, or compare the development of language using dictionaries and grammar discourses.

Religion and Philosophy

The Age of Enlightenment profoundly enriched religious and philosophical understanding and continues to influence present-day thinking. Works collected here include masterpieces by David Hume, Immanuel Kant, and Jean-Jacques Rousseau, as well as religious sermons and moral debates on the issues of the day, such as the slave trade. The Age of Reason saw conflict between Protestantism and Catholicism transformed into one between faith and logic -- a debate that continues in the twenty-first century.

Law and Reference

This collection reveals the history of English common law and Empire law in a vastly changing world of British expansion. Dominating the legal field is the *Commentaries of the Law of England* by Sir William Blackstone, which first appeared in 1765. Reference works such as almanacs and catalogues continue to educate us by revealing the day-to-day workings of society.

Fine Arts

The eighteenth-century fascination with Greek and Roman antiquity followed the systematic excavation of the ruins at Pompeii and Herculaneum in southern Italy; and after 1750 a neoclassical style dominated all artistic fields. The titles here trace developments in mostly English-language works on painting, sculpture, architecture, music, theater, and other disciplines. Instructional works on musical instruments, catalogs of art objects, comic operas, and more are also included.

The BiblioLife Network

This project was made possible in part by the BiblioLife Network (BLN), a project aimed at addressing some of the huge challenges facing book preservationists around the world. The BLN includes libraries, library networks, archives, subject matter experts, online communities and library service providers. We believe every book ever published should be available as a high-quality print reproduction; printed on-demand anywhere in the world. This insures the ongoing accessibility of the content and helps generate sustainable revenue for the libraries and organizations that work to preserve these important materials.

The following book is in the "public domain" and represents an authentic reproduction of the text as printed by the original publisher. While we have attempted to accurately maintain the integrity of the original work, there are sometimes problems with the original work or the micro-film from which the books were digitized. This can result in minor errors in reproduction. Possible imperfections include missing and blurred pages, poor pictures, markings and other reproduction issues beyond our control. Because this work is culturally important, we have made it available as part of our commitment to protecting, preserving, and promoting the world's literature.

GUIDE TO FOLD-OUTS MAPS and OVERSIZED IMAGES

The book you are reading was digitized from microfilm captured over the past thirty to forty years. Years after the creation of the original microfilm, the book was converted to digital files and made available in an online database.

In an online database, page images do not need to conform to the size restrictions found in a printed book. When converting these images back into a printed bound book, the page sizes are standardized in ways that maintain the detail of the original. For large images, such as fold-out maps, the original page image is split into two or more pages

Guidelines used to determine how to split the page image follows:

• Some images are split vertically; large images require vertical and horizontal splits.
• For horizontal splits, the content is split left to right.
• For vertical splits, the content is split from top to bottom.
• For both vertical and horizontal splits, the image is processed from top left to bottom right.

REPORT

OF THE

SECRETARY of the TREASURY

TO THE

House of Representatives,

RELATIVE TO A PROVISION

FOR THE

SUPPORT

OF THE

PUBLIC CREDIT

OF THE

UNITED STATES,

IN CONFORMITY TO A RESOLUTION OF THE TWENTY-FIRST DAY OF
SEPTEMBER, 1789

PRESENTED TO THE HOUSE ON THURSDAY THE 4th DAY OF JANUARY, 1790.

PUBLISHED BY ORDER OF THE HOUSE OF REPRESENTATIVES.

NEW-YORK
PRINTED BY FRANCIS CHILDS AND JOHN SWAINE.
M,DCC,XC.

REPORT

OF THE

SECRETARY OF THE TREASURY

TO THE

HOUSE OF REPRESENTATIVES.

TREASURY DEPARTMENT, *January* 9, 1790.

THE Secretary of the Treasury, in obedience to the resolution of the House of Representatives, of the twenty-first day of September last, has, during the recess of Congress, applied himself to the consideration of a proper plan for the support of the Public Credit, with all the attention which was due to the authority of the House, and to the magnitude of the object.

In the discharge of this duty, he has felt, in no small degree, the anxieties which naturally flow from a just estimate of the difficulty of the task, from a well-founded diffidence of his own qualifications for executing it with success, and from a deep and solemn conviction of the momentous nature of the truth contained in the resolution under which his investigations have been conducted, "That an *adequate* provision for the support of the Public Credit, is a matter of high importance to the honor and prosperity of the United States."

With an ardent desire that his well-meant endeavors may be conducive to the real advantage of the nation, and with the utmost deference to the superior judgment of the House, he now respectfully submits the result of his enquiries and reflections, to their indulgent construction.

In the opinion of the Secretary, the wisdom of the House, in giving their explicit sanction to the proposition which has been stated, cannot but be applauded by all, who will seriously consider, and trace through their obvious consequences, these plain and undeniable truths.—

That exigencies are to be expected to occur, in the affairs of nations, in which there will be a necessity for borrowing.—

That loans in times of public danger, especially from foreign war, are found an indispensable resource, even to the wealthiest of them.—

And that in a country, which, like this, is possessed of little active wealth, or in other words, little monied capital, the necessity for that resource, must, in such emergencies, be proportionably urgent.

And as on the one hand, the necessity for borrowing in particular emergencies cannot be doubted, so on the other, it is equally evident, that to be able to borrow upon *good terms*, it is essential that the credit of a nation should be well established.

For when the credit of a country is in any degree questionable, it never fails to give an extravagant premium, in one shape or another, upon all the loans it has occasion to make. Nor does the evil end here, the same disadvantage must be sustained upon whatever is to be bought on terms of future payment.

From this constant necessity of *borrowing* and *buying dear*, it is easy to conceive how immensely the expences of a nation, in a course of time, will be augmented by an unsound state of the public credit.

To attempt to enumerate the complicated variety of mischiefs in the whole system of the social œconomy, which proceed from a neglect of the maxims that uphold public credit, and justify the solicitude manifested by the House on this point, would be an improper intrusion on their time and patience.

In so strong a light nevertheless do they appear to the Secretary, that on their due observance at the present critical juncture, materially depends, in his judgment, the individual and aggregate prosperity of the citizens of the United States, their relief from the embarrassments they now experience, their character as a People, the cause of good government.

If the maintenance of public credit, then, be truly so important, the next enquiry which suggests itself is, by what means it is to be effected?——The ready answer to which question is, by good faith, by a punctual performance of contracts. States, like individuals, who observe their engagements, are respected and trusted while the reverse is the fate of those, who pursue an opposite conduct

Every breach of the public engagements, whether from choice or necessity, is in different degrees hurtful to public credit When such a necessity does truly exist, the evils of it are only to be palliated by a scrupulous attention, on the part of the government, to carry the violation no farther than the necessity absolutely requires, and to manifest, if the nature of the case admits of it, a sincere disposition to make reparation, whenever circumstances shall permit But with every possible mitigation, credit must suffer, and numerous mischiefs ensue It is therefore highly important, when an appearance of necessity seems to press upon the public councils, that they should examine well its reality, and be perfectly assured, that there is no method of escaping from it, before they yield to its suggestions For though it cannot safely be affirmed, that occasions have never existed, or may not exist, in which violations of the public faith, in this respect, are inevitable, yet there is great reason to believe, that they exist far less frequently than precedents indicate ; and are oftenest either pretended through levity, or want of firmness, or supposed through want of knowledge. Expedients might often have been devised to effect, consistently with good faith, what has been done in contravention of it Those who are most commonly creditors of a nation, are, generally speaking, enlightened men , and there are signal examples to warrant a conclusion, that when a candid and fair appeal is made to them, they will understand their true interest too well to refuse their concurrence in such modifications of their claims, as any real necessity may demand

While the observance of that good faith, which is the basis of public credit, is recommended by the strongest inducements of political expediency, it is enforced by considerations of still greater authority There are arguments for it, which rest on the immutable principles of moral obligation And in proportion as the mind is disposed to contemplate, in the order of Providence, an intimate connection between public virtue and public happiness, will be its repugnancy to a violation of those principles.

This reflection derives additional strength from the nature of the debt of the United States It was the price of liberty The faith of America has been repeatedly pledged for it, and with solemnities, that give peculiar force to the obligation There is indeed reason to regret that it has not hitherto been kept, that the necessities of the war, conspiring with inexperience in the subjects of finance, produced direct infractions , and that the subsequent period has been a continued scene of negative violation, or non-compliance. But a diminution of this regret arises from the reflection, that the last seven years have exhibited an earnest and uniform effort, on the part of the government of the union, to retrieve the national credit, by doing justice to the creditors of the nation , and that the embarrassments of a defective constitution, which defeated this laudable effort, have ceased

From this evidence of a favorable disposition, given by the former government, the institution of a new one, cloathed with powers competent to calling forth the resources of the community, has excited correspondent expectations A general belief, accordingly, prevails, that the credit of the United States will quickly be established on the firm foundation of an effectual provision for the existing debt. The influence, which this has had at home, is witnessed by the rapid increase, that has taken place in the market value of the public securities From January to November, they rose thirty-three and a third per cent, and from that period to this time, they have risen fifty per cent more. And the intelligence from abroad announces effects proportionably favourable to our national credit and consequence

It cannot but merit particular attention that among ourselves the most enlightened friends of good government are those, whose expectations are the highest.

To justify and preserve their confidence , to promote the encreasing respectability of the American name , to answer the calls of justice , to restore landed property to its due value , to furnish new resources both to agriculture and commerce , to cement more closely the union of the states , to add to their security against foreign attack , to establish public order on the basis of an upright and liberal policy —These are the great and invaluable ends to be secured, by a proper and adequate provision, at the present period, for the support of public credit

To this provision we are invited, not only by the general considerations, which have been noticed, but by others of a more particular nature. It will procure to every class of the community some important advantages, and remove some no less important disadvantages.

The advantage to the public creditors from the increased value of that part of their property which constitutes the public debt, needs no explanation.

But there is a consequence of this, less obvious, though not less true, in which every other citizen is interested. It is a well known fact, that in countries in which the national debt is properly funded, and an object of established confidence, it answers most of the purposes of money Transfers of stock or public debt are there equivalent to payments in specie ; or in other words, stock, in the principal transactions of business, passes current as specie.—The same thing would, in all probability happen here, under the like circumstances.

The benefits of this are various and obvious.—

First. Trade is extended by it, because there is a larger capital to carry it on, and the merchant can at the same time, afford to trade for smaller profits , as his stock, which, when unemployed, brings him in an interest from the government, serves him also as money, when he has a call for it in his commercial operations

Secondly Agriculture and manufactures are also promoted by it For the like reason, that more capital can be commanded to be employed in both , and because the merchant, whose enterprize in foreign trade, gives to them activity and extension, has greater means for enterprize.

Thirdly The interest of money will be lowered by it , for this is always in a ratio, to the quantity of money, and to the quickness of circulation This circumstance will enable both the public and individuals to borrow on easier and cheaper terms

And from the combination of these effects, additional aids will be furnished to labour, to industry, and to arts of every kind

But these good effects of a public debt are only to be looked for, when, by being well funded, it has acquired an *adequate* and *stable* value. Till then, it has rather a contrary tendency The fluctuation and insecurity incident to it in an unfunded state, render it a mere commodity, and a precarious one As such, being only an object of occasional and particular speculation, all the money applied to it is so much diverted from the more useful channels of circulation, for which the thing itself affords no substitute So that, in fact, one serious inconvenience of an unfunded debt is, that it contributes to the scarcity of money.

This distinction which has been little if at all attended to, is of the greatest moment. It involves a question immediately interesting to every part of the community, which is no other than this—Whether the public debt, by a provision for it on true principles, shall be rendered a *substitute* for money, , or whether, by being left as it is, or by being provided for in such a manner as will wound those principles, and destroy confidence, it shall be suffered to continue, as it is, a pernicious drain of our cash from the channels of productive industry

The effect, which the funding of the public debt, on right principles, would have upon landed property, is one of the circumstances attending such an arrangement, which has been least adverted to, though it deserves the most particular attention The present depreciated state of that species of property is a serious calamity. The value of cultivated lands, in most of the states, has fallen since the revolution from 25 to 50 per cent In those farthest south, the decrease is still more considerable Indeed, if the representations, continually received from that quarter, may be credited, lands there will command no price, which may not be deemed an almost total sacrifice

This decrease, in the value of lands, ought, in a great measure, to be attributed to the scarcity of money —Consequently whatever produces an augmentation of the monied capital of the country, must have a proportional effect in raising that value The beneficial tendency of a funded debt, in this respect, has been manifested by the most decisive experience in Great Britain

The proprietors of lands would not only feel the benefit of this increase in the value of their property and of a more prompt and better sale, when they had occasion to sell , but the necessity of selling would be, itself, greatly diminished. As the same cause would contribute to the facility of loans, there is reason to believe, that such of them as are indebted, would be able through that resource, to satisfy their more urgent creditors

It ought not however to be expected, that the advantages, described as likely to result from funding the public debt, would be instantaneous. It might require some time to bring the value of stock to its natural level, and to attach to it that fixed confidence, which is necessary to its quality as money Yet the late rapid rise of the public securities encourages an expectation, that the progress of stock to the desireable point, will be much more expeditious than could have been foreseen. And as in the mean time it will be increasing in value, there is room to conclude, that it will, from the outset, answer many of the purposes in contemplation Particularly it seems to be probable, that from creditors, who are not themselves necessitous, it will early meet with a ready reception in payment of debts, at its current price

Having now taken a concise view of the inducements to a proper provision for the public debt, the next enquiry which presents itself is, what ought to be the nature of such a provision ? This requires some preliminary discussions

It is agreed on all hands, that that part of the debt which has been contracted abroad, and is denominated the foreign debt, ought to be provided for, according to the precise terms of the contracts relating to it The discussions, which can arise, therefore, will have reference essentially to the domestic part of it, or to that which has been contracted at home, It is to be regretted, that there is not the same unanimity of sentiment on this part, as on the other.

The Secretary has too much deference for the opinions of every part of the community, not to have observed one, which has, more than once, made its appearance in the public prints, and which is occasionally to be met with in conversation. It involves this question, whether a discrimination ought not to be made between original holders of the public securities, and present possessors, by purchase. Those who advocate a discrimination are for making a full provision for the securities of the former, at their nominal value, but contend, that the latter ought to receive no more than the cost to them, and the interest. And the idea is sometimes suggested of making good the difference to the primitive possessor.

In favor of this scheme, it is alledged, that it would be unreasonable to pay twenty shillings in the pound, to one who had not given more for it than three or four. And it is added, that it would be hard to aggravate the misfortune of the first owner, who, probably through necessity, parted with his property at so great a loss, by obliging him to contribute to the profit of the person, who had speculated on his distresses.

The Secretary, after the most mature reflection on the force of this argument, is induced to reject the doctrine it contains, as equally unjust and impolitic, as highly injurious, even to the original holders of public securities,—as ruinous to public credit.

It is inconsistent with justice, because in the first place, it is a breach of contract, in violation of the rights of a fair purchaser.

The nature of the contract in its origin, is, that the public will pay the sum expressed in the security, to the first holder, or his *assignee*. The *intent*, in making the security assignable, is, that the proprietor may be able to make use of his property, by selling it for as much as it *may be worth in the market*, and that the buyer may be *safe* in the purchase.

Every buyer therefore stands exactly in the place of the seller—has the same right with him to the identical sum expressed in the security, and having acquired that right, by fair purchase, and in conformity to the original *agreement* and *intention* of the government, his claim cannot be disputed, without manifest injustice.

That he is to be considered as a fair purchaser, results from this. Whatever necessity the seller may have been under, was occasioned by the government, in not making a proper provision for its debts. The buyer had no agency in it, and therefore ought not to suffer. He is not even chargeable with having taken an undue advantage. He paid what the commodity was worth in the market, and took the risks of reimbursement upon himself. He of course gave a fair equivalent, and ought to reap the benefit of his hazard, a hazard which was far from inconsiderable, and which, perhaps, turned on little less than a revolution in government.

That the case of those, who parted with their securities from necessity, is a hard one, cannot be denied. But whatever complaint of injury, or claim of redress, they may have, respects the government solely. They have not only nothing to object to the persons who relieved their necessities, by giving them the current price of their property, but they are even under an implied condition to contribute to the reimbursement of those persons. They knew, that by the terms of the contract with themselves, the public were bound to pay to those, to whom they should convey their title, the sums stipulated to be paid to them, and, that as citizens of the United States, they were to bear their proportion of the contribution for that purpose. This, by the act of assignment, they tacitly engage to do, and if they had an option, they could not, with integrity or good faith, refuse to do it, without the consent of those to whom they sold.

But though many of the original holders sold from necessity, it does not follow, that this was the case with all of them. It may well be supposed, that some of them did it either through want of confidence in an eventual provision, or from the allurements of some profitable speculation. How shall these different classes be discriminated from each other? How shall it be ascertained, in any case, that the money, which the original holder obtained for his security, was not more beneficial to him, than if he had held it to the present time, to avail himself of the provision which shall be made? How shall it be known, whether if the purchaser had employed his money in some other way, he would not be in a better situation, than by having applied it in the purchase of securities, though he should now receive their full amount? And if neither of these things can be known, how shall it be determined whether a discrimination, independent of the breach of contract, would not do a real injury to purchasers, and if it included a compensation to the primitive proprietors, would not give them an advantage, to which they had no equitable pretension.

It may well be imagined, also, that there are not wanting instances, in which individuals, urged by a present necessity, parted with the securities received by them from the public, and shortly after replaced them with others, as an indemnity for their first loss. Shall they be deprived of the indemnity which they have endeavoured to secure by so provident an arrangement?

Questions of this sort, on a close inspection, multiply themselves without end, and demonstrate the injustice of a discrimination, even on the most subtile calculations of equity, abstracted from the obligation of contract.

The difficulties too of regulating the details of a plan for that purpose, which would have even the semblance of equity, would be found immense. It may well be doubted whether they would not be insurmountable, and replete with such absurd, as well as inequitable consequences, as to disgust even the proposers of the measure

As a specimen of its capricious operation, it will be sufficient to notice the effect it would have upon two persons, who may be supposed two years ago to have purchased, each, securities at three shillings in the pound, and one of them to retain those bought by him, till the discrimination should take place, the other to have parted with those bought by him, within a month past, at nine shillings. The former, who had had most confidence in the government, would in this case only receive at the rate of three shillings and the interest, while the latter, who had had less confidence would receive *for what cost him the same money* at the rate of nine shillings, and his representative, *standing in his place*, would be entitled to a like rate

The impolicy of a discrimination results from two considerations, one, that it proceeds upon a principle destructive of that *quality* of the public debt, or the stock or the nation, which is essential to its capacity for answering the purposes of money—that is *the security* of *transfer*, the other, that as well on this account, as because it includes a breach of faith, it renders property in the funds less valuable, consequently induces lenders to demand a higher premium for what they lend, and produces every other inconvenience of a bad state of public credit

It will be perceived at first sight, that the transferable quality of stock is essential to its operation as money, and that this depends on the idea of complete security to the transferee, and a firm persuasion, that no distinction can in any circumstances be made between him and the original proprietor

The precedent of an invasion of this fundamental principle, would of course tend to deprive the community of an advantage, with which no temporary saving could bear the least comparison

And it will as readily be perceived, that the same cause would operate a diminution of the value of stock in the hands of the first, as well as of every other holder. The price, which any man, who should incline to purchase, would be willing to give for it, would be in a compound ratio to the immediate profit it afforded, and to the chance of the continuance of his profit. If there was supposed to be any hazard of the latter, the risk would be taken into the calculation, and either there would be no purchase at all or it would be at a proportionably less price

For this diminution of the value of stock, every person, who should be about to lend to the government, would demand a compensation, and would add to the actual difference, between the nominal and the market value, an equivalent for the chance of greater decrease, which, in a precarious state of public credit, is always to be taken into the account

Every compensation of this sort, it is evident, would be an absolute loss to the government.

In the preceding discussion of the impolicy of a discrimination, the injurious tendency of it to those, who continue to be the holders of the securities, they received from the government, has been explained. Nothing need be added, on this head, except that this is an additional and interesting light, in which the injustice of the measure may be seen. It would not only divest present proprietors by purchase, of the rights they had acquired under the sanction of public faith, but it would depreciate the property of the remaining original holders

It is equally unnecessary to add any thing to what has been already said to demonstrate the fatal influence, which the principle of discrimination would have on the public credit

But there is still a point in view in which it will appear perhaps even more exceptionable, than in either of the former. It would be repugnant to an express provision of the Constitution of the United States. This provision is, that " all debts contracted and engagements entered into before the adoption of that Constitution shall be as valid against the United States under it, as under the confederation," which amounts to a constitutional ratification of the contracts respecting the debt, in the state in which they existed under the confederation. And resorting to that standard, there can be no doubt, that the rights of assignees and original holders, must be considered as equal

In exploding thus fully the principle of discrimination, the Secretary is happy in reflecting, that he is the only advocate of what has been already sanctioned by the formal and express authority of the government of the Union, in these emphatic terms—" The remaining class of creditors (say Congress in their circular address to the states, of the 26th of April 1783) is composed, partly of such of our fellow-citizens as originally lent to the public the use of their funds, or have since manifested *most confidence* in their country, by receiving transfers from the lenders, and partly of those, whose property has been either advanced or assumed for the public service. To *discriminate* the merits of these several descriptions of creditors, would be a task equally unnecessary and invidious. If the voice of humanity plead more loudly in favor of some than of others, the voice of policy, no less than of justice, pleads in favor of all. A WISE NATION will never permit those who relieve the wants of their country, or who *rely most* on its *faith*, its *firmness*, and its *resources*, when either of them is distrusted, to suffer by the event."

B

The Secretary concluding, that a discrimination, between the different classes of creditors of the United States, cannot with propriety be *made*, proceeds to examine whether a difference ought to be permitted to *remain* between them, and another description of public creditors—Those of the states individually

The Secretary, after mature reflection on this point, entertains a full conviction, that an assumption of the debts of the particular states by the union, and a like provision for them, as for those of the union, will be a measure of sound policy and substantial justice

It would, in the opinion of the Secretary, contribute, in an eminent degree, to an orderly, stable and satisfactory arrangement of the national finances

Admitting, as ought to be the case, that a provision must be made in some way or other, for the entire debt, it will follow, that no greater revenues will be required, whether that provision be made wholly by the United States, or partly by them, and partly by the states separately.

The principal question then must be, whether such a provision cannot be more conveniently and effectually made, by one general plan issuing from one authority, than by different plans originating in different authorities

In the first case there can be no competition for resources, in the last, there must be such a competition The consequences of this, without the greatest caution on both sides, might be interfering regulations, and thence collision and confusion Particular branches of industry might also be oppressed by it The most productive objects of revenue might not be particular Either these must be wholly engrossed by one side, which might lessen the efficacy of the provisions by the other, or both must have recourse to the same objects in different modes, which might occasion an injurious action upon them, beyond what they could properly bear If this should not happen, the caution requisite to avoiding it, would prevent the revenue's deriving the full benefit of each object The danger of interference and or excess would be apt to impose restraints very unfriendly to the complete command of those resources, which are the most convenient, and to compel the having recourse to others, less easy in the themselves, and less agreeable to the community

The difficulty of an effectual command of the public resources, in case of separate provisions for the debt, may be seen in another and perhaps more striking light It would then easily appear that different states, from local considerations, would in some instances have recourse to inherent objects, in others, to the same objects, in different degrees, for procuring the funds of which they stood in need It is easy to conceive how this diversity would affect the aggregate revenue of the country By the supposition, article which yielded full supply in some states, would yield nothing, or an insufficient product, in others And hence the public revenue would not derive the full benefit of those articles, from state regulation Neither could the deficiencies be made good by those of the union It is a provision of the national constitution, that "all duties, imposts and excises, shall be uniform throughout the United States." And as the general government would be under a necessity from motives of policy, of paying regard to the duty, which may have been previously imposed upon any article, though but in a single state it would be constrained, either to refrain wholly from any further imposition, upon such article, where it had been already rated as high as was proper, or to confine itself to the difference between the existing rate, and what the article would reasonably bear Thus the pre-occupancy of an article by a single state, would tend to arrest or abridge the impositions of the union on that article And as it is supposeable, that a great variety of articles might be placed in this situation, by different arrangements of the particular states, it is evident, that the aggregate revenue of the country would be likely to be very materially contracted by the plan of separate provisions

If all the public creditors receive their dues from one source, distributed with an equal hand, their interest will be the same. And having the same interests, they will unite in the support of the fiscal arrangements of the government As these, too, can be made with more convenience, where there is no competition These circumstances combined will insure to the revenue laws a more ready and more satisfactory execution

If on the contrary there are different provisions, there will be distinct interests, drawing different ways That union and concert of views, among the creditors, which in every government is of great importance to their security, and to that of public credit, will not easily not exist, but will be likely to give place to mutual jealousy and opposition And from this cause, the operation of the systems which may be adopted, both by the particular states, and by the union, with relation to their respective debts, will be in danger of being counteracted

There are several reasons, which render it probable, that the situation of the state creditors would be worse, than that of the creditors of the union, if there be not a national assumption of the state debts Of these it will be sufficient to mention two, one, that a principal branch of revenue is exclusively vested in the union, the other, that a state must always be checked in the imposition of taxes on articles of consumption, from the want of power to extend the same regulation to the other states, and from the tendency of partial duties to injure its industry and commerce. Should the state creditors stand upon a less eligible footing than the others, it is unnatural to expect they would see with pleasure a provision for them. The influence which their dissatisfaction might have, could not but operate injuriously, both for the creditors, and the credit, of the United States

Hence it is even the interest of the creditors of the union, that those of the individual states should be comprehended in a general provision. Any attempt to secure to the former either exclusive or peculiar advantages, would materially hazard their interests.

Neither would it be just, that one class of the public creditors should be more favoured than the other. The objects for which both descriptions of the debt were contracted, are in the main the same Indeed a great part of the particular debts of the States has arisen from assumptions by them on account of the union And it is most equitable, that there should be the same measure of retribution for all.

There is an objection, however, to an assumption of the state debts, which deserves particular notice It may be supposed, that it would increase the difficulty of an equitable settlement between them and the United State

The principles of that settlement wherever they shall be discussed, will require all the moderation and wisdom of the government In the opinion of the Secretary, that discussion, till further lights are obtained, would be premature

All therefore which he would now think adviseable on the point in question would be, that the amount of the debts assumed and provided for, should be charged to the respective states, to abide an eventual arrangement. This, the United States, as assignees to the creditors, would have an indisputable right to do

But as it might be of satisfaction to the House to have before them some plan for the liquidation of accounts between the union and its members, which, including the assumption of the state debts, would consist with equity The Secretary will submit in this place such thoughts on the subject as have occurred to his own mind, or been suggested to him, most compatible, in his judgment, with the end proposed

Let each state be charged with all the money advanced to it out of the treasury of the United States, liquidated according to the specie value, at the time of each advance, with interest at six per cent

Let it also be charged with the amount, in specie value, of all the securities which shall be assumed, with the interest upon them to the time, when interest shall become payable by the United States

Let it be credited for all monies paid and articles furnished to the United States, and for all other expenditures during the war, either towards general or particular defence, whether authorized or unauthorized by the United States, the whole liquidated to specie value, and bearing an interest of six per cent from the several times at which the several payments, advances and expenditures accrued

And let all sums of continental money now in the treasuries of the respective states, which shall be paid into the treasury of the United States, be credited at specie value

Upon a statement of the accounts according to these principles, there can be little doubt, that balances would appear in favor of all the states, against the United States

To equalize the contributions of the states, let each be then charged with its proportion of the aggregate of those balances, according to some equitable ratio, to be devised for that purpose

If the contributions should be found disproportionate, the result of this adjustment would be, that some states would be creditors, some debtors to the union

Should this be the case, as it will be attended with less inconvenience for the United States, to have to pay balances to, than to receive them from the particular states, it may perhaps, be practicable to effect the former by a second process, in the nature of a transfer of the amount of the debts of debtor states, to the credit of creditor states, observing the ratio by which the first apportionment shall have been made This, whilst it would destroy the balances due from the former, would increase those due to the latter These to be provided for by the United States, at a reasonable interest, but not to be transferable

The expediency of this second process must depend on a knowledge of the result of the first If the inequalities should be too great, the arrangement may be impracticable, without unduly increasing the debt of the United States. But it is not likely, that this would be the case It is also to be remarked, that though this second process might not upon the principle of apportionment, bring the thing to the point aimed at, yet it may approach so nearly to it, as to avoid essentially the embarrassment, of having considerable balances to collect from any of the states

The whole of this arrangement to be under the superintendence of commissioners, vested with equitable discretion, and final authority.

The operation of the plan is exemplified in the schedule A

The general principle of it seems to be equitable, for it appears difficult to conceive a good reason, why the expences for the particular defence of a part in a common war should not be a common charge, as well as those incurred professedly for the general defence. The defence of each part is that of the whole, and unless all the expenditures are brought into a common mass, the tendency must be, to add, to the calamities suffered, by being the most exposed to the ravages of war, an increase of burthens.

This plan seems to be susceptible of no objection, which does not belong to every other, that proceeds on the idea of a final adjustment of accounts. The difficulty of settling a ratio, is common to all. This must, probably, either be sought for in the proportions of the requisitions, during the war, or in the decision of commissioners appointed with plenary power. The rule prescribed in the Constitution, with regard to representation and direct taxes, would evidently not be applicable to the situation of parties, during the period in question.

The existing debt of the United States is excluded from the computation, as it ought to be, because it will be provided for out of a general fund.

The only discussion of a preliminary kind, which remains relates to the distinctions of the debt into principal and interest. It is well known, that the arrears of the latter bear a large proportion to the amount of the former. The immediate payment of these arrears is evidently impracticable, and a question arises, what ought to be done with them?

There is good reason to conclude, that the impressions of many are more favorable to the claim of the principal than to that of the interest, at least so far, as to produce an opinion, that an inferior provision might suffice for the latter.

But to the Secretary, this opinion does not appear to be well founded. His investigations of the subject have led him to a conclusion, that the arrears of interest have pretensions, at least equal to the principal.

The liquidated debt, traced to its origin, falls under two principal discriminations. One, relating to loans, the other to services performed and articles supplied.

The part arising from loans, was at first made payable at fixed periods, which have long since elapsed, with an early option to lenders, either to receive back their money at the expiration of those periods, or to continue it at interest, 'till the whole amount of continental bills circulating should not exceed the sum in circulation at the time of each loan. This contingency, in the sense of the contract, never happened, and the presumption is, that the creditors preferred continuing their money indefinitely at interest, to receiving it in a depreciated and depreciating state.

The other parts of it were chiefly for objects, which ought to have been paid for at the time, that is, when the services were performed or the supplies furnished, and were not accompanied with any contract for interest.

But by different acts of government and administration, concurred in by the creditors, these parts of the debt have been converted into a capital, bearing an interest of six per cent per annum, but without any definite period of redemption. A portion of the loan-office debt has been exchanged for new securities of that import. And the whole of it seems to have acquired that character, after the expiration of the periods prefixed for re-payment.

If this view of the subject be a just one, the capital of the debt of the United States, may be considered in the light of an annuity at the rate of six per cent per annum, redeemable at the pleasure of the government, by payment of the principal. For it seems to be a clear position, that when a public contracts a debt payable with interest, without any precise time being stipulated or understood for payment of the capital, that time is a matter of pure discretion with the government, which is at liberty to consult its own convenience respecting it, taking care to pay the interest with punctuality.

Wherefore, as long as the United States should pay the interest of their debt, as it accrued, their creditors would have no right to demand the principal.

But with regard to the arrears of interest, the case is different. These are now due, and those to whom they are due, have a right to claim immediate payment. To say, that it would be impracticable to comply, would not vary the nature of the right. Nor can this idea of impracticability be honorably carried further, than to justify the proposition of a new contract upon the basis of a commutation of that right for an equivalent. This equivalent too ought to be a real and fair one. And what other fair equivalent can be imagined for the detention of money, but a reasonable interest? Or what can be the standard of that interest, but the market rate, or the rate which the government pays in ordinary cases?

From this view of the matter, which appears to be the accurate and true one, it will follow, that the arrears of interest are entitled to an equal provision with the principal of the debt.

The result of the foregoing discussions is this—That there ought to be no discrimination between the original holders of the debt, and present possessors by purchase—That it is expedient, there should be an assumption of the state debts by the Union, and that the arrears of interest should be provided for on an equal footing with the principal.

The next enquiry, in order, towards determining the nature of a proper provision, respects the quantum of the debt, and the present rates of interest

The debt of the union is distinguishable into foreign and domestic.

	Dollars.	Cents.
The foreign debt as stated in the schedule B amounts to principal - bearing an interest of four, and partly an interest of five per cent	10,070,307	
Arrears of interest to the last of December, 1789, - -	1,640,071	62
Making together, dollars	11,710,378	62

The domestic debt may be sub-divided into liquidated and unliquidated, principal and interest

	Dollars	Cents.
The principal of the liquidated part, as stated in the schedule C, amounts to bearing an interest of six per cent	27,383,917	74
The arrears of interest as stated in the schedule D to the end of 1790, amount to - - - -	13,030,168	20
Making together, dollars	40,414,685	94

This includes all that has been paid in indents (except what has come into the treasury of the United States) which, in the opinion of the Secretary, can be considered in no other light, than as interest due

The unliquidated part of the domestic debt, which consists chiefly of the continental bills of credit, is not ascertained, but may be estimated at 2,000,000 dollars

These several sums constitute the whole of the debt of the United States, amounting together to 54,124,464 dollars, and 56 cents.

That of the individual states is not equally well ascertained. The schedule E shews the extent to which it has been ascertained by returns pursuant to the order of the House of the 21st September last, but this not comprehending all the states, the residue must be estimated from less authentic information. The Secretary, however, presumes, that the total amount may be safely stated at 25 millions of dollars, principal and interest. The present rate of interest of the state debts is in general, the same with that of the domestic debt of the union.

On the supposition, that the arrears of interest ought to be provided for, on the same terms with the principal, the annual amount of the interest, which, at the existing rates, would be payable on the entire mass of the public debt, would be,

	Dollars.	Cents.
On the foreign debt, computing the interest on the principal, as it stands, and allowing four per cent on the arrears of interest, - -	542,599	06
On the domestic debt, including that of the states, - -	4,044,845	15
Making together, dollars	4,587,444	81

The interesting problem now occurs. Is it in the power of the United States, consistently with those prudential considerations, which ought not to be overlooked, to make a provision equal to the purpose of funding the whole debt, at the rates of interest which it now bears, in addition to the sum which will be necessary for the current service of the government?

The Secretary will not say that such a provision would exceed the abilities of the country; but he is clearly of opinion, that to make it, would require the extension of taxation to a degree, and to objects, which the true interest of the public creditors forbids. It is therefore to be hoped, and even to be expected, that they will chearfully concur in such modifications of their claims, on fair and equitable principles, as will facilitate to the government an arrangement substantial, durable and satisfactory to the community. The importance of the last characteristic will strike every discerning mind. No plan, however flattering in appearance, to which it did not belong, could be truly entitled to confidence.

It will not be forgotten, that exigencies may, ere long, arise, which would call for resources greatly beyond what is now deemed sufficient for the current service; and that, should the faculties of the country be exhausted or even *strained* to provide for the public debt, there could be less reliance on the sacredness of the provision.

But while the Secretary yields to the force of those considerations, he does not lose sight of those fundamental principles of good faith, which dictate, that every practicable exertion ought to be made, scrupulously to fulfil the engagements of the government; that no change in the rights of its creditors ought to be attempted without their voluntary consent; and that this consent ought to be voluntary in fact, as well as in name. Consequently, that every proposal of a change ought to be in the shape of an appeal to their reason and to their interest, not to their necessities. To this end it is requisite, that a fair equivalent should be offered for what may be asked to be given up, and unquestionable security for the remainder. Without this, an alteration, consistently with the credit and honor of the nation, would be impracticable.

It remains to see, what can be proposed in conformity to these views.

C

It has been remarked, that the capital of the debt of the union is to be viewed in the light of an annuity at the rate of fix per cent. per annum, redeemable at the pleasure of the government, by payment of the principal. And it will not be required, that the arrears of interest should be confidered in a more favourable light. The fame character, in general, may be applied to the debts of the individual states.

This view of the fubject admits, that the United States would have it in their power to avail themfelves of any fall in the market rate of interest, for reducing that of the debt.

This property of the debt is favourable to the public, unfavourable to the creditor. And may facilitate an arrangement for the reduction of interest, upon the bafis of a fair equivalent.

Probabilities are always a rational ground of contract. The Secretary conceives, that there is good reafon to believe, if effectual meafures are taken to eftablifh public credit, that the government rate of interest in the United States, will, in a very fhort time, fall at least as low as five per cent, and that in a period not exceeding twenty years, it will fink ftill lower, probably to four.

There are two principal caufes which will be likely to produce this effect; one, the low rate of interest in Europe, the other, the increafe of the monied capital of the nation, by the funding of the public debt.

From three to four per cent. is deemed good interest in feveral parts of Europe. Even less is deemed fo in fome places. And it is on the decline, the increafing plenty of money continually tending to lower it. It is prefumable, that no country will be able to borrow of foreigners upon better terms, than the United States, becaufe none can, perhaps, afford fo good a fecurity. Our situation expofes us less, than that of any other nation, to thofe cafualties, which are the chief caufes of expence or incumbrances, in proportion to our real means are less, though thefe cannot immediately be brought fo readily into action, and our progrefs in refources from the early state of the country, and the immenfe tracts of unfettled territory, must neceffarily exceed that of any other. The advantages of this fituation have already engaged the attention of the European monied-interes, particularly among the Dutch. And as they become better underftood, they will have their greater influence. Hence a larger proportion of the cafh of Europe as may be wanted, will be a certain fource, in our market, for the ufe of government. And this will in it fall have the effect of a reduction of the rate of interest, not indeed to the level of the places, which fend their money to market, but to fomething much nearer to it than our prefent rate.

The influence, which the funding of the debt is calculated to have, in lowering interest, has been already remarked and explained. It is hardly poffible, that it fhould not be materially affected by fuch an increafe of the monied capital of the union, as would refult from the proper funding of feventy millions of dollars. But the probability of an increafe in the rate of interest, requires confirmation from facts, which exifted prior to the revolution. It is well known, that in fome of the states, money might with facility be borrowed, on good fecurity, at five per cent, and, not unfrequently, even at lefs.

The most enlightened of the public creditors will be most fenfible of the juftnefs of this view of the fubject, and of the propriety of the ufe which will be made of it.

The Secretary, in purfuance of it, will affume, as a probability, fufficiently great to be a ground of calculation, both on the part of the government and of its creditors—that the interest of money in the United States will, in five years, fall to five per cent. and, in twenty, to four. The probability, in the mind of the Secretary, is rather that the fall may be more rapid and more confiderable; but he prefers a mean, as most likely to engage the affent of the creditors, and more equitable in itfelf, becaufe it is predicated on probabilities, which may err on one fide, as well as on the other.

Premifing thefe things, the Secretary fubmits to the Houfe, the expediency of propofing a loan to the full amount of the debt, as well of the particular states, as of the union, upon the following terms.

Firft—That for every hundred dollars fubfcribed, payable in the debt (as well interest as principal) the fubfcriber be entitled, at his option, either

To have two thirds funded at an annuity, or yearly interest of fix per cent, redeemable at the pleafure of the government, by payment of the principal; and to receive the other third in lands in the Weftern Territory, at the rate of twenty cents per acre. Or,

To have the whole fum funded at an annuity or yearly interest of four per cent. irredeemable by any payment exceeding five dollars per annum on account both of principal and interest; and to receive, as a compenfation for the reduction of interest, fifteen dollars and eighty cents, payable in lands, as in the preceding cafe. Or

To have fixty-fix dollars and two thirds of a dollar funded immediately at an annuity or yearly interest of fix per cent irredeemable by any payment exceeding four dollars and two thirds of a dollar per annum, on account both of principal and interest; and to have, at the end of ten years, twenty-fix dollars and eighty-eight cents, funded at the like interest and rate of redemption. Or

To have an annuity for the remainder of life, upon the contingency of living to a given age, not lefs diftant than ten years, computing interest at four per cent. Or

To have an annuity for the remainder of life, upon the contingency of the survivorship of the youngest of two persons, computing interest, in this case also, at four per cent.

In addition to the foregoing loan, payable wholly in the debt, the Secretary would propose, that one should be opened for ten millions of dollars, on the following plan

That for every hundred dollars subscribed, payable one half in specie, and the other half in debt (as well principal as interest) the subscriber be entitled to an annuity or yearly interest of five per cent irredeemable by any payment exceeding six dollars per annum, on account both of principal and interest

The principles and operation of these different plans may now require explanation.

The first is simply a proposition for paying one third of the debt in land, and funding the other two thirds, at the existing rate of interest, and upon the same terms of redemption, to which it is at present subject

Here is no conjecture, no calculation of probabilities. The creditor is offered the advantage of making his interest principal, and he is asked to facilitate to the government an effectual provision for his demands by accepting a third part of the sum in land, at a fair valuation

The general price, at which the western lands have been, heretofore, sold, has been a dollar per acre in public securities; but at the time the principal purchases were made, these securities were worth, in the market, less than three shillings in the pound. The nominal price, therefore, would not be the proper standard, under present circumstances, nor would the precise specie value then given, be a just rule. Because, as the payments were to be made by instalments, and the securities were at the time of the purchases, extremely low, the probability of a moderate rise must be presumed to have been taken into the account. Twenty cents, therefore, seem to bear an equitable proportion to the two considerations of value at the time and likelihood of increase.

It will be understood, that upon this plan, the public retains the advantage of availing itself of any fall in the market rate of interest, for redeeming so much upon the debt, which is perfectly just, as no present sacrifice, either in the quantum of the principal, or in the rate of interest, is required from the creditor

The inducement to the measure is, the payment of one third of the debt in land

The second plan is grounded upon the supposition, that interest, in five years, will fall to five per cent in fifteen more, to four. As the capital remains entire, but bearing an interest of four per cent only, compensation is to be made to the creditor, for the interest of two per cent per annum for five years, and of one per cent per annum, for fifteen years, to commence at the distance of five years. The present value of these two sums or annuities, computed according to the terms of the supposition, is, by strict calculation, fifteen dollars and seventy hundred and ninety-two thousandth parts of a dollar; a fraction less than the sum proposed

The inducement to the measure here is the reduction of interest to a rate, more within the compass of a convenient provision; and the payment of the compensation in lands

The inducements to the individual are—the accommodation afforded to the public—the high probability of a complete equivalent—the chance even of gain, should the rate of interest fall, either more speedily or in a greater degree, than the calculation supposes. Should it fall to five per cent sooner than five years, should it fall lower than five before the additional fifteen were expired, or should it fall below four, previous to the payment of the debt, there would be, in each case, an absolute profit to the creditor. As his capital will remain entire, the value of it will increase, with every decrease of the rate of interest

The third plan proceeds upon the like supposition of a successive fall in the rate of interest. And upon that supposition offers an equivalent to the creditor. One hundred dollars, bearing an interest of six per cent for five years, of five per cent for fifteen years, and thenceforth of four per cent (these being the successive rates of interest in the market) is

equal to a capital of - - 122 dollars, 510725 parts,

bearing an interest of four per cent which, converted into a capital, bearing a fixed rate of interest of six per cent, is equal to - - 81 dollars, 6738166 parts.

The difference between sixty-six dollars and two thirds of a dollar (the sum to be funded immediately) and this last sum is - - 15 dollars, 0172 parts,

which at six per cent per annum, amounts at the end of ten years, to 26 dollars, 8755 part, the sum to be funded at the expiration of that period

It ought, however, to be acknowledged, that this calculation does not make allowance for the principle of redemption, which the plan itself includes; upon which principle the equivalent in a capital of six per cent would be by strict calculation, 87 dollars, 50766 parts.

But there are two considerations which induce the Secretary to think, that the one proposed would operate more equitably than this. One is, that it may not be very early in the power of the United States to avail themselves of the right of redemption reserved in the plan. The other is, that with regard to the part to be funded at the end of ten years, the principle of redemption is suspended during that time, and the full interest at six per cent. goes on *improving* at the *sum* rate, which for the *laſt five years* will exceed the market rate of intereſt, according to the ſuppoſition

The equivalent is regulated in this plan, by the circumſtance of fixing the rate of intereſt higher, than it is ſuppoſed it will continue to be in the market, permitting only a gradual diſcharge of the debt, in an eſtabliſhed proportion, and conſequently preventing advantage being taken of any decreaſe of intereſt below the ſtipulated rate

Thus the true value of eighty-one dollars and ſixty-ſeven cents, the capital propoſed, conſidered as a perpetuity, and bearing ſix per cent intereſt, when the market rate of intereſt was five per cent would be a ſmall fraction more than ninety-eight dollars, when it was four per cent would be one hundred and twenty-two dollars and fifty-one cents   But the propoſed capital being ſubject to gradual redemption, it is evident, that its value, in each caſe, would be ſomewhat leſs. Yet from this may be perceived, the manner in which a leſs capital at a fixed rate of intereſt, becomes an equivalent for a greater capital, at a rate liable to variation and diminution

It is preſumable, that thoſe creditors, who do not entertain a favorable opinion of property in weſtern lands, will give a preference to this laſt mode of modelling the debt   The Secretary is ſincere in affirming, that, in his opinion, it will be likely to prove, *to the full* as beneficial to the creditors, as a proviſion for his debt upon its preſent terms.

It is not intended, in either caſe to oblige the government to redeem, in the proportion ſpecified, but to ſecure to it, the right of doing ſo, to avoid the inconvenience of a perpetuity

The fourth and fifth plans abandon the ſuppoſition which is the baſis of the two preceding ones, and offer only four per cent. throughout

The reaſon of this is, that the payment being deferred, there will be an accumulation of compound intereſt, in the intermediate period againſt the public, which, without a very provident adminiſtration, would turn to its detriment   And the ſuſpenſion of the burthen would be too apt to beget a relaxation of efforts in the mean time   The meaſure therefore, its object being temporary accommodation, could only be adviſeable upon a moderate rate of intereſt

With regard to individuals, the inducement will be ſufficent at four per cent   There is no diſpoſition of money, in private loans, making allowance for the uſual delays and caſualties, which would be equally beneficial as a future proviſion

A hundred dollars advanced upon the life of a perſon of eleven years old, would produce an annuity*

<table>
<tr><td></td><td>Dollars</td><td>Parts</td></tr>
<tr><td>If commencing at twenty-one, of</td><td>10</td><td>346</td></tr>
<tr><td>If commencing at thirty-one, of</td><td>18</td><td>803</td></tr>
<tr><td>If commencing at forty-one, of</td><td>37</td><td>286</td></tr>
<tr><td>If commencing at fifty-one, of</td><td>78</td><td>580</td></tr>
</table>

The ſame ſum advanced upon the chance of the ſurvivorſhip of the yongeſt of two lives, one of the perſons being twenty-five, the other, thirty years old, would produce, if the youngeſt of the two, ſhould ſurvive, an annuity + for the remainder of life of   23 dollars,   556 parts

From theſe inſtances may readily be diſcerned, the advantages, which theſe deferred annuities afford, for ſecuring a comfortable proviſion for the evening of life, or for wives, who ſurvive their huſbands.

The ſixth plan alſo relinquiſhes the ſuppoſition, which is the foundation of the ſecond, and third, and offers a higher rate of intereſt upon ſimilar terms of redemption, for the conſideration of the payment of one half of the loan in ſpecie.   This is a plan highly advantageous to the creditors, who may be able to make that payment, while the ſpecie itſelf could be applied in purchaſes of the debt, upon terms, which would fully indemnify the public for the increaſed intereſt.

It is not improbable, that foreign holders of the domeſtic debt, may embrace this as a deſireable arrangement

As an auxiliary expedient, and by way of experiment, the Secretary would propoſe a loan upon the principles of a tontine ‡

To conſiſt of ſix claſſes, compoſed reſpectively of perſons of the following ages :

  Firſt claſs, of thoſe of 20 years and under
  Second claſs, of thoſe above 20, and not exceeding 30.
  Third claſs, of thoſe above 30, and not exceeding 40.
  Fourth claſs, of thoſe above 40, and not exceeding 50.
  Fifth claſs, of thoſe above 50, and not exceeding 60.
  Sixth claſs, of thoſe above 60.

* *See Schedule* F.
† *Table Schedule* G.
‡ *See Table Schedule* H.

Each share to be two hundred dollars. The number of shares in each class, to be indefinite. Persons to be at liberty to subscribe on their own lives, or on those of others, nominated by them.

	Dollars.	Cents.
The annuity upon a share in the first class to be - - -	8	40
upon a share in the second - - - -	8.	65
upon a share in the third - - - -	9.	0
upon a share in the fourth - - - -	9.	65
upon a share in the fifth - - - -	10	70
upon a share in the sixth - - - -	12	80

The annuities of those who die, to be equally divided among the survivors, until four-fifths shall be dead, when the principle of survivorship shall cease, and each annuitant thenceforth enjoy his dividend as a several annuity during the life, upon which it shall depend.

These annuities are calculated on the best life in each class, and at a rate of interest of four per cent. with some deductions in favor of the public. To the advantages which these circumstances present, the cessation of the right of survivorship on the death of four-fifths of the annuitants, will be no inconsiderable addition.

The inducements to individuals are, a competent interest for their money from the outset, secured for life, and the prospect of continual increase, and even of large profit to those, whose fortune it is, to survive their associates.

It will have appeared, that in all the proposed loans, the Secretary has contemplated the putting the interest upon the same footing with the principal. That on the debt of the United States, he would have computed to the last of the present year. That on the debt of the particular states, to the last of the year 1791, the reason for which distinction will be seen hereafter.

In order to keep up a due circulation of money, it will be expedient, that the interest of the debt should be paid quarter-yearly. This regulation will, at the same time, conduce to the advantage of the public creditors, giving them, in fact, by the anticipation of payment, a higher rate of interest, which may, with propriety, be taken into the estimate of the compensation to be made to them. Six per cent. per annum, paid in this mode, will truly be worth six dollars, and one hundred and thirty five thousandths parts of a dollar, computing the market interest at the same rate.

The Secretary thinks it adviseable, to hold out various propositions, all of them compatible with the public interest, because it is, in his opinion, of the greatest consequence, that the debt should, with the consent of the creditors, be remoulded into such a shape, as will bring the expenditure of the nation to a level with its income. 'Till this shall be accomplished, the finances of the United States will never wear a proper countenance. Arrears of interest, continually accruing, will be as continual a monument, either of inability, or of ill faith, and will not cease to have an evil influence on public credit. In nothing are appearances of greater moment, than in whatever regards credit. Opinion is the soul of it, and this is affected by appearances, as well as realities. By offering an option to the creditors, between a number of plans, the change meditated will be more likely to be accomplished. Different tempers will be governed by different views of the subject.

But while the Secretary would endeavour to effect a change in the form of the debt, by new loans, in order to render it more susceptible of an adequate provision, he would not think it proper to aim at procuring the concurrence of the creditors by operating upon their necessities.

Hence whatever surplus of revenue might remain, after satisfying the interest of the new loans, and the demand for the current service, ought to be divided among those creditors, if any, who may not think fit to subscribe to them. But for this purpose, under the circumstance of depending propositions, a temporary appropriation will be most adviseable, and the sum must be limited to four per cent. as the revenues will only be calculated to produce, in that proportion, to the entire debt.

The Secretary confides for the success of the propositions, to be made, on the goodness of the reasons upon which they rest, on the fairness of the equivalent to be offered in each case, on the discernment of the creditors of their true interest, and on their disposition to facilitate the arrangements of the government, and to render them satisfactory to the community.

The remaining part of the task to be performed is, to take a view of the means of providing for the debt, according to the modification of it, which is proposed.

On this point the Secretary premises, that, in his opinion, the funds to be established, ought, for the present, to be confined to the existing debt of the United States; as well, because a progressive augmentation of the revenue will be most convenient, as because the consent of the state creditors is necessary, to the assumption contemplated, and though the obtaining of that consent may be inferred with great assurance, from their obvious interest to give it, yet 'till it shall be obtained, an actual provision for the debt, would be premature. Taxes could not, with propriety, be laid for an object, which depended on such a contingency.

D

All that ought now to be done, refpecting it, is, to put the matter in an effectual train for a future provifion For which purpofe, the Secretary will, in the courfe of this report, fubmit fuch propofitions, as appear to him advifeabl .

The Secretary now proceeds to a confideration of the neceffary funds.

It has been ftated that the debt of the United States confifts of

	Dollars	Cents
The foreign debt, ar oun ing, with arrears of interest, to -	11,710,378	62
And the domeftic debt amount , with like arrears, computed to the end of the year 1790, to - - -	42,414,085	94
Making together, Dollars	54,124,464	56

The intereft on the domeftic debt is computed to the end of this year, becaufe the details of carrying any plan into execution, will exhauft the year

	Dollars	Cents.
The annual intereft of the foreign debt has been ftated at	542,599	66
And the intereft on the domeftic debt at four per cent would amount to	1,696,563	43
Making together, dollars,	2,239,163	09

Thus to pay the intereft of the foreign debt, and to pay four per cent on the whole of the domeftic debt, principal and intereft, forming a new capital,

will require a yearly income of - - 2,239,163 dollars, 9 cents

The fum which, in the opinion of the Secretary, ought now to be provided in addition to what the current fervice will require

For, though the rate of intereft, propofed by the third plan, exceeds four per cent on the whole debt, and the annuities on the tontine will alfo exceed four per cent on the fums which may be fubfcribed ; yet, as the actual provifion for a part is, in the former cafe, fufpended ; as meafures for reducing the debt, by purchafes, may be advantageoufly purfued, and as the payment of the deferred annuities will of courfe be poftponed, four per cent on the whole, will be a fufficient provifion

With regard to the inftalments of the foreign debt, thefe, in the opinion of the Secretary, ought to be paid by new loans abroad Could funds be conveniently fpared, from other exigencies, for paying them, the United States could ill bear the drain of cafh, at the prefent juncture, which the meafure would be likely to occafion.

But to the fum which has been ftated for payment of the intereft, muft be added a provifion for the current fervice This the Secretary eftimates at fix hundred thoufand dollars , * making, with the amount of the intereft, two millions, eight hundred and thirty-nine thoufand, one hundred and fixty-three dollars, and nine cents

This fum may, in the opinion of the Secretary, be obtained from the prefent duties on imports and tonnage, with the additions, which, without any poffible difadvantage either to trade, or agriculture, may be made on wines, fpirits, including thofe diftilled within the United States, teas and coffee.

The Secretary conceives, that it will be found policy, to carry the duties upon articles of this kind, as high as will be confiftent with the practicability of a fafe collection This will leffen the neceffity, both of having recourfe to direct taxation, and of accumulating duties where they would be more inconvenient to trade, and upon objects, which are more to be regarded as neceffaries of life.

That the articles which have been enumerated, will, better than moft others, bear high duties, can hardly be a queftion They are all of them, in reality—luxuries—the greateft part of them foreign luxuries , fome of them, in the excefs in which they are ufed, pernicious luxuries And there is, perhaps, none of them, which is not confumed in fo great abundance, as may, juftly, denominate it, a fource of national extravagance and impoverifhment The confumption of ardent fpirits particularly, no doubt very much on account of their cheapnefs, is carried to an extreme, which is truly to be regretted, as well in regard to the health and the morals, as to the œconomy of the community.

Should the increafe of duties tend to a decreafe of the confumption of thofe articles, the effect would be, in every refpect defireable The faving which it would occafion, would leave individuals more at their eafe, and promote a more favourable balance of trade As far as this decreafe might be applicable to diftilled fpirits, it would encourage the fubftitution of cyder and malt liquors, benefit agriculture, and open a new and productive fource of revenue.

It is not however, probable, that this decreafe would be in a degree, which would fruftrate the expected benefit to the revenue from raifing the duties Experience has fhewn, that luxuries of every kind, lay the ftrongeft hold on the attachments of mankind, which, efpecially when confirmed by habit, are not eafily alienated from them.

* See Schedule I.

The same fact affords a security to the merchant, that he is not likely to be prejudiced by confiderable duties on fuch articles. They will ufually command a proportional price. The chief things in this view to be attended to, are, that the terms of payment be fo regulated, as not to require inconvenient advances, and that the mode of collection be fecure.

To other reafons, which plead for carrying the duties upon the articles which have been mentioned, to as great an extent as they will well bear, may be added thefe, that they are of a nature, from their extenfive confumption, to be very productive, and are amongft the moft difficult objects of illicit introduction.

Invited by fo many motives to make the beft ufe of the refource, which thefe articles afford, the effential enquiry is—in what mode can the duties upon them be moft effectually collected?

With regard to fuch of them, as will be brought from abroad, a duty on importation recommends itfelf by two leading confiderations, one is, that meeting the object at its firft entrance into the country, the collection is drawn to a point, and fo far fimplified, the other is, that it avoids the poffibility of interference between the regulations of the United States, and thofe of the particular ftates.

But a duty, the precautions for the collection of which fhould terminate with the landing of the goods, as is effentially the cafe in the exifting fyftem, could not, with fafety, be carried to the extent, which is contemplated.

In that fyftem, the evafion of the duties depends, as it were, on a fingle rifk. To land the goods in defiance of the vigilance of the officers of the cuftoms, is almoft, the fole difficulty. No future purfuit, is material ally to be apprehended. And where the inducement is equivalent to the rifk, there will be found too many, who are willing to run it. Confequently there will be extenfive frauds of the revenue, againft which the utmoft rigor of penal laws, has proved, as often as it has been tried, an ineffectual guard.

The only expedient which has been difcovered, for conciliating high duties with a fafe collection, is, the eftablifhment of a fcond, or interior fcrutiny.

By purfuing the article, from its importation, into the hands of the dealers in it, the rifk of detection is fo greatly inhanced, that few, in comparifion, will venture to incur it. Indeed every dealer, who is not himfelf the fraudulent importer, then becomes in fome fort, a centinel upon him.

The introduction of a fyftem, founded on this principle, in fome fhape or other, is, in the opinion of the Secretary, effential to the efficacy of every attempt, to render the revenues of the United States equal to their exigences, their fafety, their profperity, their honor.

Nor is it lefs effential to the intereft of the honeft and fair trader. It might even be added, that every individual citizen, befides his fhare in the general weal, has a particular intereft in it. The practice of fmuggling never fails to have one of two effects, and fometimes unites them both. Either the fmuggler underfells the fair trader, as, by faving the duty, he can afford to do, and makes it a charge upon him, or he fells at the increafed price occafioned by the duty, and defrauds every man, who buys of him, of his fhare of what the public ought to receive. For it is evident, that the lofs falls ultimately upon the citizens, who muft be charged with other taxes to make good the deficiency, and fupply the wants of the ftate.

The Secretary will not prefume, that the plan, which he fhall fubmit to the confideration of the houfe, is the beft that could be devifed. But it is the one, which has appeared to him freeft from objections of any, that has occurred of equal efficacy. He acknowledges too, that it is fufceptible of improvement, by other precautions in favor of the revenue, which he did not think it expedient to add. The chief outlines of the plan are not original, but it is no ill recommendation of it, that it has been tried with fuccefs.

The Secretary accordingly propofes,

That the duties heretofore laid upon wines, diftilled fpirits, teas and coffee, fhould, after the laft day of May next, ceafe, and that inftead of them, the following duties be laid —

Upon every gallon of Madeira Wine, of the quality of London particular, thirty-five cents.

Upon every gallon of other Madeira Wine, thirty cents.

Upon every gallon of Sherry, twenty-five cents.

Upon every gallon of other Wine, twenty cents.

Upon every gallon of diftilled Spirits, more than ten per cent. below proof, according to Dicas's hydrometer, twenty cents.

Upon every gallon of thofe Spirits under five, and not more than ten per cent. below proof, according to the fame hydrometer, twenty-one cents.

Upon every gallon of thofe Spirits of proof, and not more than five per cent. below proof, according to the fame hydrometer, twenty-two cents.

Upon every gallon of thofe Spirits above proof, but not exceeding twenty per cent. according to the fame hydrometer, twenty-five cents.

Upon every gallon of those Spirits more than twenty, and not more than forty per cent. above proof, according to the same hydrometer, thirty cents

Upon every gallon of those Spirits more than forty per cent. above proof, according to the same hydrometer, forty cents

Upon every pound of Hyson Tea, forty cents

Upon every pound of other Green Tea, twenty-four cents

Upon every pound of Souchong and other black Teas, except Bohea, twenty cents.

Upon every pound of Bohea Tea, twelve cents

Upon every pound of Coffee, five cents

That upon Spirits distilled within the United States, from Molasses, Sugar, or other foreign materials, there be laid—

Upon every gallon of those Spirits, more than ten per cent below proof, according to Dicas's hydrometer, eleven cents

Upon every gallon of those Spirits under five and not more than ten per cent below proof, according to the same hydrometer, twelve cents

Upon every gallon of those Spirits of proof, and not more than five per cent below proof, according to the same hydrometer, thirteen cents

Upon every gallon of those Spirits, above proof, but not exceeding twenty per cent according to the same hydrometer, fifteen cents

Upon every gallon of those Spirits more than twenty, and not more than forty per cent above proof, according to the same hydrometer, twenty cents

Upon every gallon of those Spirits more than forty per cent above proof, according to the same hydrometer, thirty cents

That upon Spirits distilled within the United States, in any city, town or village, from materials the growth or production of the United States, there be paid—

Upon every gallon of those Spirits more than ten per cent below proof, according to Dicas's hydrometer, nine cents

Upon every gallon of those Spirits under five, and not more than ten per cent below proof, according to the same hydrometer, ten cents

Upon every gallon of those Spirits of proof, and not more than five per cent below proof, according to the same hydrometer, eleven cents

Upon every gallon of those Spirits above proof, but not exceeding twenty per cent according to the same hydrometer, thirteen cents

Upon every gallon of those Spirits more than twenty, and not more than forty per cent above proof, according to the same hydrometer, four teen cents

Upon every gallon of those Spirits, more than forty per cent above proof, according to the same hydrometer, twenty five cents

That upon all Stills employed in distilling Spirits from materials of the growth or production of the United States, in any other place, than a city, town or village, there be paid the yearly sum of sixty cents, for every gallon, English wine measure, of the capacity of each Still, including its head

The Secretary does not distribute the duties on Teas into different classes, as has been done in the impost act of the last session, because this distribution depends on considerations of commercial policy, not of revenue. It is sufficient, therefore, for him to remark, that the rates, above specified, are proposed with reference to the lowest class

The Secretary conceiving that he could not convey an accurate idea of the plan contemplated by him, for the collection of these duties, in any mode so effectual as by the draft of a bill for the purpose, begs leave respectfully to refer the House to that which will be found annexed to this report, relative to the article of distilled spirits, and which, for the better explanation of some of its parts, is accompanied with marginal remarks

It would be the intention of the Secretary, that the duties on wines should be collected upon precisely the same plan with that on imported spirits

But with regard to teas and coffee, the Secretary is inclined to think, that it will be expedient, by an essence that evince the propriety of going further, to exclude the ordinary right of the officers to visit and inspect the places in which those articles may be kept. The other precautions, which are these, will afford, though not complete, considerable security

It will not escape the observation of the House, that the Secretary, in the plan submitted, has taken the most serious care, that those citizens upon whom it is immediately to operate, be secured from every species of injury by the misconduct of the officers to be employed. These are not only strong guards against their being guilty of abuses of authority, they are not only punishable criminally, for any they may commit, and made answerable in damages to individuals, for whatever prejudice these may sustain by their acts or neglects. But even where abuses are made with probable cause, if there be an acquittal of the article seized a compensation to the proprietors for the injury their property may suffer, and even for its detention, is to be made out of the public treasury.

So solicitous indeed has the Secretary been, to obviate every appearance of hardship, that he has even included a compensation to the dealers for their agency in aid of the revenue.

With all these precautions to manifest a spirit of moderation and justice on the part of the government. And when it is considered, that the object of the proposed system is the firm establishment of public credit, that on this depends the character, security and prosperity of the nation; that advantages in every light important, may be expected to result from it, that the immediate operation of it will be upon an enlightened class of citizens, zealously devoted to good government, and to a liberal and enlarged policy, and that it is peculiarly the interest of the virtuous part of them to co-operate in whatever will restrain the spirit of illicit traffic, there will be perceived to exist the justest ground of confidence, that the plan, if eligible in itself, will experience the chearful and prompt acquiescence of the community.

The Secretary computes the nett product of the duties proposed in this report at about one million seven hundred and three thousand four hundred dollars, according to the estimate in the schedule K, which if near the truth will, together with the probable product of the duties on imports and tonnage complete the sum required. But it will readily occur, that in so unexplored a field there must be a considerable degree of uncertainty in the data. And that on this account, it will be prudent to have an auxiliary resource for the first year, in which the interest will become payable, that there may be no possibility of disappointment to the public creditors, and there may be an opportunity of providing for any deficiency, which the experiment may discover. This will accordingly be attended to.

The proper appropriation of the funds provided and to be provided, seems next to offer itself to consideration.

On this head, the Secretary would propose that the duties on distilled spirits, should be applied in the first instance, to the payment of the interest of the foreign debt.

That reserving out of the residue of those duties an annual sum of six hundred thousand dollars, for the current service of the United States, the surplus, together with the product of the other duties, be applied to the payment of the interest on the new loan by an appropriation, co-extensive with the duration of the debt.

And that if any part of the debt should remain unsubscribed, the excess of the revenue be divided among the creditors of the unsubscribed part, by a temporary disposition, with a limitation however, to four per cent.

It will hardly have been unnoticed, that the Secretary has been thus far silent on the subject of the post office. The reason is, that he has had in view the application of the revenue arising from that source, to the purposes of a sinking fund. The post-master-general gives it as his opinion that the immediate product of it, upon a proper arrangement, would probably be, not less than one hundred thousand dollars. And from its nature, with good management, it must be a growing, and will be likely to become a considerable fund. The post-master general is now engaged in preparing a plan,* which will be the foundation of a proposition for a new arrangement of the establishment. This, and some other points relative to the subject referred to the Secretary, he begs leave to reserve for a future report.

Persuaded as the Secretary is, that the proper funding of the present debt, will render it a national blessing. Yet he is so far from acceding to the position, in the latitude in which it is sometimes laid down, that "public debts are public benefits," a position inviting to prodigality, and liable to dangerous abuse,—that he ardently wishes to see it incorporated, as a fundamental maxim in the system of public credit of the United States, that the creation of debt should always be accompanied with the means of extinguishment. This he regards as the true secret for rendering public credit immortal. And he presumes, that it is difficult to conceive a situation, in which there may not be an adherence to the maxim. At least he feels an unfeigned solicitude, that this may be attempted by the United States, and that they may commence their measures for the establishment of credit, with the observance of it.

Under this impression, the Secretary proposes, that the nett product of the post office, to a sum not exceeding one million of dollars, be vested in commissioners, to consist of the Vice President of the United States or President of the Senate, the Speaker of the House of Representatives, the Chief Justice, Secretary of the Treasury and Attorney-General of the United States, for the time being, in trust, to be applied, by them, or any three of them, to the discharge of the existing public debt, either by purchases of stock in the market, or by payments on account of the principal

* The plan, since the framing of this report, has been received, and will be shortly submitted.

L

is shall appear to them most adviseable, in conformity to the public engagements, to continue to effect, until the whole of the debt shall be discharged.

As an additional expedient for effecting a reduction of the debt, and for other purposes which will be mentioned, the Secretary would further propose that the same commissioners be authorised, with the approbation of the President of the United States, to borrow, on their credit, a sum, not exceeding twelve millions of dollars, to be applied,

First. To the payment of the interest and instalments of the foreign debt, to the end of the present year, which will require 3,491,923 dollars, and 46 cents.

Secondly. To the payment of any deficiency which may happen in the product of the funds provided for paying the interest of the domestic debt.

Thirdly. To the effecting a change in the form of such part of the foreign debt, as bears an interest of five per cent. It is conceived, that, for this purpose, a new loan, at a lower interest, may be combined with other expedients. The remainder of this part of the debt, after paying the instalments, which will accrue in the course of 1790, will be 3,888,888 dollars, and 81 cents.

Fourthly. To the purchase of the public debt at the price it shall bear in the market, while it continues below its true value. This measure, which would be, in the opinion of the Secretary, highly dishonorable to the government, if it were to precede a provision for funding the debt, would become altogether unexceptionable, after that had been made. Its effect would be in favor of the public creditors, as it would tend to raise the value of stock. And all the difference, between its true value, and the actual price, would be so much clear gain to the public. The payment of foreign interest on the capital to be borrowed for this purpose, should that be a necessary consequence, would not, in the judgment of the Secretary, be a good objection to the measure. The saving by the operation would be itself, a sufficient indemnity, and the employment of that capital, in a country situated like this, would much more than compensate for it. Besides, if the government does not undertake this operation, the same inconvenience, which the objection in question supposes, would happen in another way, with a circumstance of aggravation. As long, at least, as the debt shall continue below its proper value, it will be an object of speculation to foreigners, who will not only receive the interest, upon what they purchase, and remit it abroad, as in the case of the loan, but will reap the additional profit of the difference in value. By the government's entering into competition with them, it will not only reap a part of this profit itself, but will contract the extent, and lessen the extra profit of foreign purchases. That competition will accelerate the rise of stock, and whatever greater rate this obliges foreigners to pay, for what they purchase, is so much clear saving to the nation. In the opinion of the Secretary, and contrary to an idea which is not without patrons, it ought to be the policy of the government, to raise the value of stock to its true standard as fast as possible. When it arrives to that point, foreign speculations (which, till then, must be deemed pernicious, further than as they serve to bring it to that point) will become beneficial. Their money laid out in this country upon our agriculture, commerce and manufactures, will produce much more to us, than the income they will receive from it.

The Secretary contemplates the application of this money, through the medium of a national bank, for which, with the permission of the House, he will submit a plan in the course of the session.

The Secretary now proceeds, in the last place, to offer to the consideration of the House, his ideas, of the steps, which ought at the present session, to be taken, towards the assumption of the state debts.

These are briefly, that concurrent resolutions of the two Houses, with the approbation of the President, be entered into, declaring in substance,

That the United States do assume, and will at the first session in the year 1791, provide, on the same terms with the present debt of the United States, for all such part of the debts of the respective states, or any of them, as shall, prior to the first day of January in the said year 1791, be subscribed towards a loan to the United States, upon the principles of either of the plans, which shall have been adopted by them, for obtaining a re-loan of their present debt.

Provided that the provision to be made as aforesaid, shall be suspended, with respect to the debt, of any state, which may have exchanged the securities of the United States for others issued by itself, until the whole of the said securities shall, either be re exchanged, or surrendered to the United States.

And provided also, that the interest upon the debt assumed, be computed to the end of the year 1791, and that the interest to be paid by the United States, commence on the first day of January, 1792.

That the amount of the debt of each state so assumed and provided for, be charged to such state in account with the United States, upon the fame principles, upon which it fhall be lent to the United States

That fubfcriptions be opened for receiving loans of the faid debts at the fame times and place, and under the like regulations, as fhall have been prefcribed in relation to the debt of the United States

The Secretary has now completed the objects, which he propofed to himfelf, to comprife in the prefent report He has, for the moft part, omitted details, as well to avoid fatiguing the attention of the Houfe, as becaufe more time would have been defirable even to digeft the general principles of the plan If there fhould be found right, the particular modifications will readily fuggeft themfelves in the progrefs of the work

The Secretary, in the views which have directed his purfuit of the fubject, has been influenced, in the firft place, by the confideration, that his duty from the very terms of the refolution of the Houfe, obliged him to propofe what appeared to him an adequate provifion for the fupport of the public credit, adapted at the fame time to the real circumftances of the United States, and in the next, by the reflection, that meafures which will not bear the teft of future unbiaffed examination, can neither be productive of individual reputation, nor (which is of much greater confequence) public honor, or advantage

Deeply impreffed, as the Secretary is, with a full and deliberate conviction, that the eftablifhment of public credit, upon the bafis of a fatisfactory provifion, for the public debt, is, under the prefent circumftances of this country, the true defideratum towards relief from individual and national embarrafments, that without it, thefe embarrafments will be likely to prefs ftill more feverely upon the community—He cannot but indulge an anxious wifh, that an effectual plan for that purpofe may, during the prefent feffion, be the refult of the united wifdom of the legiflature.

He is fully convinced, that it is of the greateft importance, that no further delay fhould attend the making of the requifite provifion, not only, becaufe it will give a better impreffion of the good faith of the country, and will bring earlier relief to the creditors, both which circumftances are of great moment to public credit but, becaufe the advantages to the community, from raifing ftock, as fpeedily as poffible, to its natural value, will be incomparably greater, than any that can refult from its continuance below that ftandard No profit, which could be derived from purchafes in the market, on account of the government, to any practicable extent, would be an equivalent for the lofs, which would be fuftained by the purchafes of foreigners, at a low value Not to repeat, that governmental purchafes, to be honorable, ought to be preceded by a provifion Delay, by diffeminating doubt, would fink the price of ftock, and as the temptation to foreign fpeculations, from the lownefs of the price, would be too great to be neglected, millions would probably be loft to the United States

All which is humbly fubmitted

ALLXANDER HAMILION, Secretary of the Treafury.

Suppofititious Statement of Accounts betwe

STATES.	Ratio.	Balances due to the states respectively.	Proportion of each state of the aggregate of thofe balances according to the ratio.	Balances against certain States.	Balances in favor of certain states.	Proportion of each state in the aggregate of the balances against certain states.
New-Hampfhire	?	57,500	60,000	2,500		3,000
Maffachufetts	8	180,000	160,000		20,000	8,000
Rhode-Ifland	1	20,000	20,000			1,000
Connecticut	5	110,000	100,000		10,000	5,000
New-York	6	135,000	120,000		15,000	6,000
New-Jerfey	4	72,500	80,000	7,500		4,000
Pennfylvania	8	170,000	160,000		10,000	8,000
Delaware	1	30,000	20,000		10,000	1,000
Maryland	6	110,000	120,000	10,000		6,000
Virginia	10	187,500	200,000	12,500		10,000
North-Carolina	5	90,000	100,000	10,000		5,000
South-Carolina	5	87,500	100,000	12,500		5,000
Georgia	3	50,000	60,000	10,000		3,000
	65	1,300,000	1,300,000	65,000	65,000	65,000

EXPLAN

THE firft column fuppofes a Ratio according to the prefent rule of reprefentation
The fecond column exhibits the balances which, on the principles of the ftatement fugg
The third column fhews the apportionment of the aggregate of thofe balances according
The fourth column fhews the balances againft fome States in confequence of this app
The fifth column fhews the balances in favor of fome States, in confequence of the fan
This compleats the firft Procefs propofed.

THE fecond Procefs propofed is illuftrated by the fixth and feventh columns.
The fixth fhews the fhare of each State, according to the ratio given in the amount o
The feventh fhews the ultimate balances in favor of certain States, crediting them fo

Ultimate balances in favor of certain ftates upon the principle of an extinguifhment of the balances owing by the debtor ftates, and a proportional allowance to the other ftates, adjufted according to the ratio given, and to be paid by the United States.

500
28,000
1,000
15,000
21,000
18,000
11,000

94,500

[A T I O N.

refted are fuppofed to be due to the feveral States.
ᵣto the ratio given among the States.
ᵣrtionment.
ᵢe apportionment.

f the balances againft the Debtor States.
r their propoi tions of the balance due from the Debtor States.

[SCHEDULE B]

A GENERAL STATEMENT of the FOREIGN LOANS, shewing in Abstract, the Capital Sums borrowed, and the Arrearages of Interest to the 31st December, 1789.

CAPITAL SUMS Borrowed		Livres.	Dollars. Cts.
Of the Royal French Treasury, on Interest at 5 per cent.	-	24,000,000	
In Holland, guaranteed by the French Court, at 4 per cent.	-	10,000,000	
	Livres,	34,000,000	6 295,296
Of the Royal Spanish Treasury, at 5 per cent.	-		174,011
Lenders in Holland,		Florins.	
First Loan, 5 per cent.	-	5,000,000	
Second ditto, 4 per cent.	-	2,000,000	
Third ditto, 5 per cent.	-	1,000,000	
Fourth ditto, 5 per cent.	-	1,000,000	
	Florins,	9,000,000	3,600,000
	Capital,	- -	10,070,307

ARREARAGES of INTEREST to 31st December, 1789.

On the French Loan.

			Livres		Dollars Cts.
1789, Jan 1, Five Years Interest on the	6,000,000	at 5 per cent	277,777 77
Sept 3, Six do	on the	18,000,000	do	990,999 96
Nov 5, Four do	on the	10,000,000	4 per cent	296,296.

On the Spanish Loan

ARREARAGES on the Spanish Loan of 174,011 Dollars, to 21st March, 1782, at 5 per cent	-	-	5,093 27
March 21, Seven Years Interest on do	-	-	60,904 62
			1,640,071 62
		Total Dollars,	11,710,378 62

NOTE There were certain parts of the Capital of the Dutch guaranteed Loan of 10,000,000 Florins, and of the French Loan of 18,000,000 Livres, which became due at the following periods, and remain unpaid, viz.

					Dollars Cts.
1787	Sept 3, First Payment of the 18,000,000.	1,500,000	277 777 77
	Nov 5, First do of the 10,000,000.	1,000,000	185,185 19
1788	Sept. 3, Second do. of the 18,000,000	the same	462,962 96
	Nov 5, Second do. of the 10,000,000		
1789.	Sept 3, Third do. of the 18,000,000.	the same.	462,962 96
	Nov 5, Third do. of the 10,000,000.		
		Dollars,	1,388,888 88

TREASURY DEPARTMENT, *Register's Office*, 31st Dec 1789.

JOSEPH NOURSE, Register.

To the ARREARAGE of INTEREST to 31st December, 1789, above stated,

Amounting to 1,640,071. 62

Add one year's Interest from 1st January, to 31st December, 1789, on 186,427, dollars, and 69 cents, being the Amount Principal Sum due to foreign officers, employed in the service of the United States, which Interest is annually payable at the House of Mont Grand Banker at Paris, at 6 per cent - - 11,185 66

ARREARAGES of INTEREST to 31st December, 1789, - Dollars, 1,651,257. 28

THE above Addition was adverted to, after the conclusion of the Report, but as it makes no material difference, an alteration in consequence of it, is deemed unnecessary.

ALEXANDER HAMILTON, Secretary of the Treasury.

[SCHEDULE C]

ABSTRACT of the LIQUIDATED and LOAN-OFFICE DEBT of the United States, on the 3d March, 1789

	Dollars. 90ths
REGISTERED DEBT,	4,598,462 78
Credits given to sundries on the treasury books, by virtue of special acts of Congress, which are not yet put on the Funded Debt,	187,578 65
Certificates issued by the commissioner of army accounts, deducting, both which have been cancelled and registered,	7,967,109 73
Certificates issued by the commissioners of the five departments of state, the certificates have been cancelled and registered,	903,574 53
Certificates issued by the state commissioners, deducing those which have been cancelled and registered	3,291,156 97
Loan-office certificates prior to 1781, not expressed as specie value, deducting those which have been cancelled and registered,	112,704 15
Loan-office certificates, not on terms, reduced to specie value agreeably to the scale of Congress by taking the period of the loan, viz. 3,757,900 loaned to the Secretary,	Dollars. 90ths
	3,757,900
from 1777 till March 1778,	3,550,572
1779, and the close of the loan-offices,	5,146,330
	11,463,800
Deduct specie amount cancelled and registered,	365,082
	15 11,097,818 73
Foreign officers, amount to their credit, the interest whereof is payable at the loan-office or Grand Bank at Paris, and recarried to the debit of account interest,	186,427 69
From which deduct the sums received into the Treasury on account of loans and other property, and cancelled,	28,244,833 21
	960,915 44
Leaves the amount of the domestic debt, Dollars,	27,383,917 67

* On the certificates issued between the 1st September 1777 and 1st March 1778, interest is payable on the nominal sum (being 3,759,000 dollars) although the specie value of the principal is only 2,550,572 dollars.

Register's-office, March 3, 1789,

JOSEPH NOURSE, Register

TREASURY DEPARTMENT, *Register's-office, January 1, 1790*

The above estimate was formed to the expiration of the late government—Some variation hath since taken place in several parts, without making any material alteration in the aggregate amount of the domestic debt. This arises from a daily exchange at the Treasury of Loan-office and Final Settlement Certificates, for Treasury Certificates given as evidence of the registered debt, whereby the increase of the latter is carried on in proportion to the cancelment of the former.

JOSEPH NOURSE, Register

[SCHEDULE D]

An ESTIMATE of all the INTEREST which will accrue on the DOMESTIC DEBT of the United States, from its formation to the 31st December 1790, of such partial payments as have been made on account thereof, and of the balance which will remain to be provided for, to pay up the interest fully to that period

	Dollars Cts.
THE total amount of interest arising on the loan office debt, from the opening of the several offices in 1776, to the 31st of December, 1790,	9,534,478
The total amount of interest arising on the army debt, from the several periods of its drawing interest, to the 31st December, 1790,	5,105,099
The total amount of interest arising on certificates issued by the thirteen state commissioners, estimated at	2,146,799
The total amount of interest arising on certificates issued by the commissioners for the commissary, quarter-master, marine, clothing and hospital departments, estimated at	737,338
The total amount of interest arising on the debt registered at the treasury, estimated at	396,646
The total amount of interest on debt entered in the treasury books, but for which certificates have not been issued by the Register, so as to become a part of the registered debt, estimated at	80,936
Total	17,991,296

From this total amount of interest the following deductions are to be made, viz.	Doll. Cts.	
So much paid on the loan-office debt in old emission, equal to	300,368 30	
In new emissions, to specie	96,155 49	
In indents of interest, a ditto,	1,605,992	
So much paid by the several states, paid into the treasury on account of their quotas on the orders requisitions of the late Congress,	2,044,823 35	
So much paid by the state of New Jersey to their own citizens, on the demand of so, permitted in the feveral acts or laws,	424,442 22	
So much paid by the state of South-Carolina, being two years interest on 222,865 dollars, and 61 cents, the amount of certificates issued to the line of that state at 6 per cent is	26,695 73	
Total amount of interest paid,	4,771,103 5	
Deduct these several amount less, estimated on the foregoing on 760,915 dollars, and 33 sevens, being so much of the capital of the domestic debt received in payment for lands and other public property,	172,994 75	
Total amount of deductions,		4,944,127 80

Leaves a balance of thirteen million and thirty thousand one hundred sixty eight dollars, and 20 cents, which will accrue on the domestic debt, and for which provision is to be made to pay the interest fully up to the 31st December, 1790, ... 13,030,168 20

It is to be observed, that as the certificates which have been issued for the principal of a debt of more than twenty-seven millions of dollars, are in themselves exceedingly numerous, and that as the several certificates bear in date or from different periods, it has not been practicable to form a statement of arrearages, but by ascertaining in the most accurate manner, the different periods of time from which the several parts of the domestic debt bear interest, and therefrom calculating the interest to 31st December, 1790

TREASURY DEPARTMENT, *Register's Office*, 31st December, 1789

JOSEPH NOURSE, Register.

[SCHEDULE E]

ABSTRACT of the PUBLIC DEBT of the STATES undermentioned, agreeably to statements transmitted in pursuance of the resolution of the House of Representatives of the 21st of September, 1789.

MASSACHUSETTS   *Dollars. Cents.*

Principal with interest to the 1st day of Nov 1789. £ 1,548,040 7 9 Lawful

Due to sundries for which no certificates have yet been issued,   -   20,000

Total   £ 1,568,040 7 9 at 6s per Dol   5,226,801. 29

CONNECTICUT

Principal bearing interest from the 1st of Feb 1789,   560,404

To which ought to be added for balance of state bills emitted in the year 1780, bearing interest at 5 per cent to the 1st March 1785, estimated at   24,948

Total, £ 585,352 0 0 at 6s per Dol   1,951,173 33⅓

NEW-YORK

Principal and interest computed to the 1st day of January 1790,   -   -   1,032,616 2 0

From which ought to be deducted for amount of principal and interest of continental securities loaned to the state in pursuance of their act of the 18th day of April 1786, estimated at   -   565,569

Leave for state debt proper,   -   £ 467,030 2 0 at 8s per Dol   1,167,575 25

NEW-JERSEY

Principal unredeemed,   -   295,755 4 11 at 7/6 per Dol. 788,680. 65⅓

VIRGINIA

Principal of domestic debt,   -   1,063,296 17 1

Ditto of foreign debt with interest to the 1st January 1790,   40,926 1 1

Total, £ 1,104,222 18 2 at 6s per Dol   3,680,743 25

SOUTH-CAROLINA.

Principal of domestic debt,   -   1,069,652 2 4

Indents of interest on ditto in circulation,   71,325 7 2

Foreign debt, principal and interest, due to the 1st of January 1789,   -   115,810 0 1

Total, £ 1,256,787 9 7 at 4/3 per Dol   5,386,232. 5

Total dollars, 18,201,205 60⅔

It will be observed, that the period to which interest is calculated on the debts abovementioned is only specified with accuracy on the statements which have been transmitted from Massachusetts, Connecticut and New-York. From the best information which the Secretary can obtain, he presumes—That in the statement made of the debt of New-Jersey, interest has been calculated to the 31st day of December 1788. That on the debt of Virginia, interest has been calculated to the 31st day of December 1788. On that of South-Carolina, to the 1st day of April 1790.

From the states of New-Hampshire, Pennsylvania, Delaware, Maryland, North-Carolina and Georgia, no accounts of their respective state debts have been forwarded.

The Secretary is however of opinion from the result of enquiries made by him—That the state debt of New-Hampshire may be estimated at about   Dollars 300,000

That the state debts *proper* of Pennsylvania (that is exclusive of their assumption of the continental debt) at about   Dollars 2,200,000

And that of Maryland, at   Ditto 800,000

From the above statement and estimates, the amount of principal and interest of the state debts (exclusive of Delaware, North-Carolina, Georgia and Rhode Island) appears to be about twenty one millions and a half, but as the debts of the four last states are not included in the above sum and it is possible that a greater arrearage of interest may be due on the state debts than is at present ascertained, the aggregate of the principal and interest may be computed at twenty-five millions of dollars.

ALEXANDER HAMILTON, *Secretary of the Treasury.*

COMMONWEALTH OF MASSACHUSETTS.

A Statement of the Debt of the Commonwealth of Maſſachuſetts, as it reſpects the notes iſſued by the ſeveral Treaſurers, to the firſt of November, 1789.

	£	s	d
November 1, 1789, excluſive of half pay notes,	1,403,459	16	11
Notes iſſued to widows and orphan children of the deceaſed officers of the late continental army, for the ſeven years half pay, agreeable to reſolves of Congreſs, - - - -	8,246	11	10

	£	s	d
Intereſt on the foregoing notes ſince October, 1781,	579,660	6	4
Of which has been paid - -	443,326	7	4

	£	s	d
Intereſt remaining due, November 1, 1789, - -	136,333	19	0
	£.1,548,040	7	9

Remains due on the books of the committee for ſettling with the late continental army, to the widows and orphan children of deceaſed officers of ſaid army, and to officers and ſoldiers for their ſervices, about - 20,000

N B By an act of the legiſlature, one third part of the revenue of Exciſe is appropriated to pay the exigencies of government, and the other two third parts for the payment of intereſt of the notes, which pays about one quarter part of the intereſt, the other three quarters are unprovided for

Treaſury-Office, Boſton, October 31, 1789

ALEXANDER HODGDON, Treaſurer.

COMPARED with the original, in the office of the Secretary of the Treaſury
WILLIAM DUER

STATE OF CONNECTICUT

A Statement of the Public Debt of the State of Connecticut, as it ſtood November 1, 1789

	£	s	d
Notes iſſued to the Connecticut line payable June 1, 1782, -	2,334	13	11½
Ditto - ditto - 1783, -	2,339	13	4
Ditto - ditto - 1784, -	3,252	12	1
Ditto - ditto - 1785, -	42,519	6	1½
Ditto - ditto - 1786, -	28,189	6	3½
Ditto - ditto - 1787, -	28,448	5	6¼
Ditto - ditto - 1788, -	21,593	5	4¼
Ditto - ditto - 1789, -	20,097	5	7¾
Ditto dated February 1, 1781, iſſued per act of Aſſembly, Nov 1780,	153,229	8	6½
Ditto of various dates, ditto per act of ditto, May, 1781,	33,947	11	8½
Ditto dated June 1, 1781, ditto ditto, for remounting dragoons,	1,932	8	0
Ditto of various dates, ditto ditto, May, 1783,	41,841	6	1½
Ditto iſſued per act of May, 1789, for old notes re-loaned, -	180,890	1	0
	560,404	18	9½
Notes iſſued per particular acts of Aſſembly, payable out of civil liſt funds,	2,856	11	4
Certificates for intereſt, &c iſſued on the ſtate debt, up to February 1, 1789, and remaining unpaid November 1, 1789, - -	19,140	3	9¾
Balance of orders unpaid, drawn by Oliver Wolcott, Eſq payable out of the 1/ tax, granted in January 1783, - -	692	8	10
Balance of ſtate bills, which were emitted in March, June and July, 1780, with the intereſt at 5 per cent to the 1ſt of March, 1785, eſtimated at	24,948	9	1

There are a number of pay table orders drawn on former taxes, the amount, ſuppoſed not great, cannot be aſcertained.

There is alſo out-ſtanding, a ſum of old emiſſions of paper, iſſued before the war—the amount unknown.

[28]
```

ACCOUNT of LOAN-OFFICE and FINAL SETTLEMENT CERTIFICATES in the treasury of the State
of CONNECTICUT

| | | | | | |
|---|---|---|---|---|---|
| Loan-office certificates, | - | - | - | £ 442 | 19 | 7 |
| Final settlement certificates, | - | - | - | 2,151 | 17 | 1 |
| | | | | £ 2,594 | 16 | 8 |

Amount of interest certificates that were issued upon the evidence of the United
States debt, received by the treasurer of the state of Connecticut for taxes and
impost duties, and delivered to William Imlay, Esq continental loan-officer, from
January 0, 1786, to November 1, 1789, - - £ 33,996 15 3
COMPARED with the original in the office of the Secretary of the Treasury.

A STATEMENT of the FUNDS provided for the payment of the principal and interest of the public
debt of the state of CONNECTICUT

BALANCES of taxes laid for the payment of interest on the state debt, and the first three classes
of army notes, as appears from the treasury books, November 1, 1789, being the balance of fifteen
taxes including abatements, collecting fees, &c. - £ 40,489 14 10
Balance of excise and impost bonds payable, including collecting fees, &c 9,070 15 2
A tax of four pence on the pound, laid on the list, 1788, amounting to
£ 1,452 860 10 11 for the payment of interest on the state debt, and the
balance of the three first classes of the state notes, the nett avails estimated at 20,266 14 4
A tax of eight pence on the pound, on the same list, laid for the payment
of the balance of state bills, orders on 2s 6d and 1s taxes, and part of the
principal of the state debt ; the nett avails estimated at - 40,533 8 8
Excise for the payment of interest on the state debt, &c estimated at 5,000 0 0
The first article in the above statement of funds will probably, upon settlement of those old
taxes, fall greatly short of the sum set down, to say how much, is merely conjectural There will
also be loss upon the excise and impost bonds The amount of the excise for the current year is
very uncertain

*Comptroller's-Office, 1st December, 1789.*

RALPH POMEROY, Comptroller

---

STATE of NEW-YORK.
A STATEMENT of the DEBT of the State of NEW-YORK.

The following species of Certificates, &c have been issued by the State, and are still unredeemed, viz.

| | Principal Sum, Spec val. | | | Interest to Jan 1, 1792 | | |
|---|---|---|---|---|---|---|
| Certificates for Money loaned, pursuant to resolutions of the 4th day of April, 1778, | £. 111 | 13 | 3 | £ 78 | 14 | 5 |
| for do pursuant to a law of the 30th of June, 1780, - | 741 | 6 | 0 | 422 | 10 | 9 |
| for horses purchased in the year 1780, | 904 | 5 | 0 | 515 | 8 | 5 |
| for depreciation of pay to the army dated 31st July, 1780, - | 54,520 | 1 | 7 | 25,669 | 17 | 4 |
| for pay of the year 1781, to do dated the 1st January, 1782, - | 17,972 | 6 | 9 | 8,626 | 14 | 0 |
| for pensions to widows of military officers, | 8,104 | 18 | 2 | 3,647 | 4 | 2 |
| for pay of levies, militia, &c &c | 42,871 | 4 | 3 | 18,220 | 5 | 3 |
| for other certificates received on loan, pursuant to a law passed the 18th April, 1786, - - | 523,848 | 5 | 1 | 144,058 | 5 | 4 |
| for four-fifths of the interest due on those received on loan, - | 105,669 | 9 | 8 | | | |
| for claims on forfeited estates | 25,897 | 8 | 10 | 3,884 | 12 | 3 |
| Bills of credit, called New Emission, emitted pursuant to a law passed the 30th of June, 1780, bearing interest, - - - | 3,612 | 16 | 0 | 1,174 | 3 | 1 |
| Ditto, emitted pursuant to resolutions of Congress, and Convention of this State, reduced to specie value, | 1,047 | 0 | 0 | | | |
| | £. 785,300 | 14 | 7 | £ 206,297 | 15 | 0 |

There are large demands against forfeited estates, un-
liquidated, and others liquidated, for which no cer-
tificates have yet issued, to the amount of 41,017 12 5
```

There are no funds specially provided for redeeming the aforesaid Certificates, except the following, viz.

The arrears of old taxes may probably produce about	-	£ 10,000 0 0
Quit rents, about		20,000 0 0

Fifteen townships of new lands, or 375,000 acres, ordered to be sold (by a law passed the 25th February, 1789,) and are now surveying

GERARD BANCKER, *Treasurer of the State of New-York.*

New-York, November 30, 1789

An ACCOUNT of CONTINENTAL SECURITIES now in the Treasury of the State of NEW-YORK, viz.

		Principal	Int 1st Jan 1790.
Certificates issued by William Barber,	-	£ 352,471 13 1	£ 105,741 9 11
Ditto, by loan-officers in this State,		277,418 16 4	83,234 12 11
Ditto, by John Pierce, Burrall, Denning, Bindon, and Fox,	-	290,614 4 5	89,884 5 4
Interest facilities,	-	2,702 14 8	
		£ 932,037 8 6	£ 278,860 8 2

OF the above-mentioned Loan-Office and Barber's Certificates, the sum of £ 470,649 17 6 was received in on loan by the State in 1786, and one fifth of the interest that was due thereon, to the 31st December, 1784, then paid, and certificates for the remaining four fifths issued, payable in one year, of which certificates three fourths remain unredeemed, as represented in the former part of this statement

GERARD BANCKER, *Treasurer of the State of New-York.*

New-York, November 30, 1789

COMPARED with the Original in the office of the Secretary of the Treasury.

An ACCOUNT of CERTIFICATES due from the UNITED STATES to the INHABITANTS of the State of NEW-JERSEY, which draw interest at the TREASURY.

	Principal	Annual Interest.
1st Continental loan-office certificates, - £	420,511 0 10	25,230 13 3
2d Certificates issued by John Pierce, commissioner, for arrears of pay, &c - - -	147,118 15 2¼	8,827 2 6
3d. Certificates by Benjamin Thompson, Commissioner,	344,237 11 2	20,654 5 0
£	911,867 7 2¼	54,712 0 9

COMMUTATION

4th Certificates issued by John Pierce, Commissioner, and given to the officers of the late Jersey line, for their commutation, - - - - -	66,899 2 6	

STATE DEBT

1st. Certificates given to the officers and soldiers of the late Jersey line, for the depreciation of their pay, of which there was outstanding October 1, 1786, - -	99,526 11 4	
2d Ditto given by the Commissioners in the several counties for militia pay, of which there was outstanding October 1, 1786,	55,565 17 7½	
3d Certificates given by Silas Condict, Commissioner,	121,521 8 7	
4th Ditto given by the Treasurer and Auditor for demands against confiscated estates, - -	32,020 2 9	
5th Ditto issued by the Auditor for militia pay, -	821 4 7¼	
	£ 309,255 4 11	
Paid into the Treasury since October 1786,	13,500 0 0	
	£ 295,755 4 11	
Annual interest of state debt, -		£ 17,745 6 3½

COMPARED with the Original in the Office of the Secretary of the Treasury.

ABSTRACT of the PUBLIC DEBTS due from the State of VIRGINIA.

ON intereſt { Army debt for pay and depreciation of the officers and ſoldiers,	£.936,830	7	6
at 6 per cent { Loan-office debt, - - -	119,382	7	4
{ Certificates iſſued for the paper money funded,	7,183	2	3

Balance due to Foreign creditors, including the intereſt (at 6 per cent) to the 1ſt of January, 1790, on £ 9,415 0 2 part of the ſaid balance, for which warrants have not been drawn by the creditors, - - 40,826 1 1

JOHN PENDLETON, Auditor of Public Accounts.

Virginia, Auditor's-Office, November 20, 1789

COMPARED with the original in the office of the Secretary of the Treaſury

---

The Auditor-General reports the following STATEMENT of the DEBT due by the State of
SOUTH-CAROLINA, viz

PRINCIPAL INDENTS

BALANCE iſſued from the treaſury of the ſtate aforeſaid, and yet remaining to be iſſued on the 1ſt of October, 1789, - - £ 1,069,652 2 4½

To be cancelled by

Balance of bonds for confiſcated property,	£ 79,985	10	0½			
Purchaſes of ditto, unſettled for, -	12,910	0	0			
Balance of amerciaments, -	7,713	4	6			
Ditto for bonds for public property -	35,065	10	6			
Ditto of lands granted to 1ſt November, 1789,	42,568	1	7½	178,242	6	8

Balance ſtill to be cancelled, Sterling, £ 891,409 15 8½

SPECIAL INDENTS

Amount iſſued, and to be iſſued, - - -		£ 440,368	0	0
Deduct, for ſo much received into the treaſury, - -		369,042	12	9½

Balance in circulation, and yet to be iſſued, £ 71,325 7 2½

Agreeably to a report of the committee of ways and means, the debts due to the State for the arrears of taxes, &c. are ſufficient to cancel the above balance

FOREIGN DEBT

Amount due to ſundry perſons, - - -						£ 93,244	17	4
Balance of intereſt due 1ſt January, 1789, -		£ 29,558	4	11½				
Deduct, for ſo much paid J S Cripps, agent, £ 4,949 5 4½								
Balance paid to ſuch creditors as were here or their attorneys, -	2,043	16	10	6,993	2	2½	22,565	2	9

Principal and balance due 1ſt January, 1789, £ 115,810 0 1

FUNDS appropriated by the Legiſlature.

Out of the taxes payable the 1ſt April, 1790, -	£ 10,000		
Intereſt on the paper medium, to 1ſt May, 1791, -	12,750		
Balance of bonds given for confiſcated property, payable in ſpecie,	1,610	17	3½
The ſums due, and that ſhall become due, for amercements, in ſpecie, - - -	8,371	16	6
Balance of bonds given for duties, payable by inſtalments,	6,240	14	3
Bonds for duties due prior to 1ſt Jan. 1788, not inſtalled,	233	3	4½
A tax of 1-4th of a dollar per head, per annum, on all negroes, muſtizoes, and mulattoes, for ten years, from February 1791, the number computed to be about 100,000, which will amount to - - -	58,333	6	8

Sterling, £ 97,539 18 0½

J. McCALL, Auditor.

Auditor's-Office, Charleſton, 30th *November,* 1789.

COMPARED with the original in the office of the Secretary of the Treaſury

(SCHEDULE F)

TABLE shewing the Annuity which a person of a given age, would be entitled to during life, from the time he should arrive at a given age, upon the present payment of a hundred dollars, computing Interest at four per cent.

Age	Annuity	Age	Annuity	Age	Annuity	Age	Annuity
1 21	23 453	31 42	625	41 8 1	522	50	174 11
2 22	20 376	32 37	365	42 7 1	936	50	143 14
3 23	19 415	33 35	77	43 72	4 05	50	128 46
4 24	18 826	34 3	970	44 71	697	50	117 64
5 25	18 457	35 34	060	45 7	540	50	108 95
6 26	18 282	36 34	619	46 72	584	50	101 60
7 27	18 18	37 34	767	47 73	752	50	95 210
8 28	18 258	38 35	235	48 75	720	50	89 971
9 29	18 382	39 35 8	9	49 78	025	50	85 238
10 30	18 617	40 37	6	50 81	965		
11 31	19 316	41 18 8c		41 3	286	50	75 500
12 32	19 4	42 19 072		42 38	162	50	73 258
13	19 519	33 19 82		43 39	249		70 246
14 24	1 668	34 19 70		44 40	493		66 279
15 25	10 727	35 20 058		45 41	638	50	63 151
16 26	10 813	36 20 489		46 42	957	50	60 129
17 27	10 939	37 20 911		47 44	355	50	57 258
18 28	11 065	38 21 354		48 45	888	50	54 520
19 29	11 195	39 21 821		49 47	519	50	51 907
20 30	11 352	40 22 3135		50 49	415		
21 31	11 515	41 22 836		50 47	038		
22 32	11 687	42 23 386		50 44	770		
23 33	11 846	43 23 987		50 42	534		
24 34	12 028	44 24 719		50 40	460		
25 35	12 253	45 25 396		50 38	510		
26 36	12 462	46 26 128		50 36	572		
27 37	12 682	47 26 902		50 34	726		
28 38	12 913	48 27 749		50 32	967		
29 39	13 155	49 28 647		50 31	329		
30 40	13 385			50 29	643		
31 41	13 629			50 28	073		
32 42	13 884			50 26	580		
33 43	14 190			50 25	161		
34 44	14 547			50 23	812		
35 45	14 827			50 22	483		
36 46	15 157			50 21	217		
37 47	15 512			50 20	023		
38 48	15 896			50 18	886		
39 49	16 301			50 17	806		
40 50	16 783						

(SCHEDULE G)

TABLE shewing what Annuity would be enjoyed by the Survivor of any two persons of certain ages, for the remainder of life after the determination of the life in expectation, upon the present payment of one hundred dollars, computing Interest at four per cent, and the duration of life according to Doctor Halley's Tables.

Age of the eldest	Annuity of Survivor	Age of the youngest	Annuity of Survivor	Age of the eldest	Annuity of Survivor	Age of the eldest	Annuity of Survivor
10	28 248	20 28 (10)		28 555		45	30 62
15	26 392	25 26 04		30 26 501		50	27 005
20	24 545	30 23 923		40 23 496		55	23 375
25	22 716	35 21 753		45 21 061		60 20	040
30	20 920	40 19 825	30.5	18 739		65	16 957
35	10 1683	45 17 576		5 16 529		70	1 40
10 45	17 264	5 16 013		60 14 484			
5	15 8 7	55 14 201		65 12 600		50	22 164
50	14 263	60 12 620		70 10 894		55	7 731
55	12 78	65 11 100				50 60	513
60	11 237	7 9 707		35 28 993		65	19 662
65	10 99			4 10 114		70	16 357
70	8 905	25 27 816		5 3 331			
		3 25 556		5 22 702		55	34 286
15	28 169	35 23 331	5	8 172		60 28 543	
20	26 198	40 21 159		6 15 820	55	6 23 742	
25	24 219	45 19 247		65 13 666		70	19 175
30	22 276	25 50 17 0 0		70 11 72		60	37 509
35	20 370	55 15 117				60 65 30 4 3	
40	18 523	60 13 330		40 29 673		7	24 044
15 45	16 750	65 11 689		45 26 469			
5	15 053	70 10 173		50 23 337		65	42 481
55	12 963			55 20 354	65	70 32 679	
60	11 948			6 17 604			
65	10 553			65 15 060	70	70 50 994	
7	9 270			70 12 799			

To find the Annuity upon the Survivorship of the youngest of any two lives, expressed in this table, look for the respective ages under their respective heads, and opposite the number, which corresponds with the age of the eldest will be seen the Annuity required

G

[SCHEDULE II]

TABLE for a TONTINE of Six Classes; the number of lives in each class being indefinite, calculated on a payment of two hundred dollars by each subscriber, and at a rate of interest of four per cent. The computation on the best life in each class, and on the supposition that the subscribers to each class will not be less than the respective numbers specified in the first column.

Number of lives in each Class	Ages	Annuity which it will entitle to	Dividends at successive periods during the probable continuance of Life					
			At the expiration of 10 years	At the expiration of 20 years	At the expiration of 30 years	At the expira- tion of 40 years	At the expira- tion of 50 years	At the expira- tion of 50 ye.
75	1 to 20	8,261	9,724	11,400	14,042	18,041	25,278	40,130	121,577
65	20 to 30	8,676	10,222	12,606	16,314	23,116	30,613	48,660	
50	31 to 40	9,266	11,162	14,366	20,354	34,890	142,282		
41	41 to 50	9,650	12,183	17,605	30,326	100,150			
31	51 to 60	10,714	14,173	26,020	91,068				
24	61 to 72	12,822	20,518	71,804					

This Table, which is calculated on so small a number of persons, will serve to shew the greatness of the advantage to the fortunate survivors, in case of a numerous subscription.

[SCHEDULE I]

GENERAL ESTIMATE for the Services of the Current Year

Civil List, as per No 1,	-	-	254,892 73
War department, No 2,	-	-	155,537 72
Military Pensions, No 3,	-	-	96,979 72
		Dollars,	507,410 17

With an eye to the necessary provisions for the foreign department, and to other arrangements which may be found requisite, it appeared advisable to state in the report, to which this is annexed, a sum of six hundred thousand dollars for the current service.

Treasury Department, January 5, 1790.

[No I]

ESTIMATE of the Expenditure for the Civil List of the United States, on the present establishment for the year 1790.

			Dollars.
For the compensation to the President of the United States,	-	-	25,000
That of the Vice President,	-		5,000
Compensation to the Chief Justice,			4,000
Ditto to each of the five Associate Justices, 3500 dollars each,			17,500
To the Judges of the following Districts, viz			
District of Maine,			1,000
New-Hampshire,		-	1,000
Massachusetts,	-	-	1,200
Connecticut,	-	-	1,000
New-York,	-	-	1,500
New-Jersey,	-	-	1,000
Pennsylvania,	-	-	1,500
Delaware,	-	-	800
Maryland,	-		1,500
Virginia,			1,800
Kentuckey,	-		1,000
South-Carolina,	-	-	1,800
Georgia,	-	-	1,500
Attorney-General,	-	-	1,500
Carried forward,			69,700

	Dols	C's.	Dols	C s.
Brought forward,	69 700			

Compensation to the members of Congress,
during the attendance of the whole number for six months, viz

Speaker of the House of Representatives, at twelve dollars per day,	2,190			
Twenty members, at six dollars per day,	87,600			
Travelling expences computed,	15000			
		104 700		
To the Secretary of the Senate, one year's salary,	1,500			
Additional allowance estimated for six months, at two dollars per day,	365	1,865		
Principal Clerk to the Secretary of the Senate, for same time, at three dollars per day,		547 50		
Engrossing Clerk to the Secretary of the Senate, estimated for same time, at two dollars per day,		365		
Chaplain to the Senate, estimated for six months, at five hundred dollars per annum,		250		
Compensation to the door keeper of the Senate, for the same time, at three dollars per day,		547 50		
Messenger to the Senate, for the same time, at 2 dollars per day,		365		
Clerk of the House of Representatives, for one year's		1 50		
Additional allowance calculated for six months, at two dollars per day,	365	1,365		
Principal Clerk in the office of do. estimated for same time, at three dollars per day,		547 50		
Engrossing Clerk for same time, estimated at two dollars per day,		365		
Chaplain to the House of Representatives, estimated for same time, at five hundred dollars per annum,		250		
Serjeant at arms, estimated for same time at 2 dols per day,		730		
Door-keeper, for same time, at 3 dollars per day,		547 50		
Assistant door-keeper for do. at 2 dollars per day,		365	183,100	

TREASURY DEPARTMENT

Secretary of the Treasury,	-	-	3,500
Assistant of the Secretary of the Treasury,		-	1,500
Five Clerks, at 500 dollars per annum each,		-	2,500
Messenger and office keeper,		-	150
Comptroller of the Treasury,	-	-	2,000
Principal Clerk to do			800
Four Clerks, at 500 dollars each,		-	2,000
Treasurer,			2,000
Principal Clerk to do	-		600
Auditor of the Treasury,	-	-	1,500
Principal Clerk to do	-	-	600
Twelve Clerks to do who, besides the current business under the New Government, has the settlement of the accounts which arose under the Confederation, in the quarter-master, commissary, clothing, hospital, and marine departments, and ordnance stores, and also the accounts of the secret and commercial committees of Congress, at 500 dollars each,			6,000
Register of the Treasury	-	-	1,250
One Clerk on the books of the public creditors, called Funded Debt at the Treasury, transfers, &c			500
One Clerk in the office of the Register, employed in keeping the accounts of interest arising on the domestic debt,			500
One do on the principal books of the treasury, in journalizing and posting into the ledger,	-	-	500
			25,850

Carried forward,			208,950

	Dol. Cts	Dol. Cts
Brought forward,		205,95
One Clerk in copying fair statements of the public accounts, and other transcripts as required from the treasury books,	500	
One do in keeping the accounts of the register, figned and fealed, &c for ships tranfmitted to the collectors of the cuftoms at the feveral ports, filing duplicates of regifters iffued by the collectors, keeping the accounts of the transfers of veffels, and other butinefs of record, arifing from Act for regiftering of veffels, regulating the coafting trade, and other purpofes therein mentioned,	500	
Two do on the old accounts of the treafury, and books and accounts of the thirteen late ftate commiffioners, at five hundred dollars each,	1,000	
Meffenger and office keeper to the comptroller, auditor and regifter's office,	150	150

DEPARTMENT OF STATE

Secretary of that department,	3,500	
Chief Clerk,	800	
Three Clerks, at 500 dollars each,	1,500	
Meffenger and office keeper,	150	5,950

DEPARTMENT OF WAR

Secretary of the department,	3,000	
Chief Clerk	600	
Two Clerks at five hundred dollars each,	1,000	
Meffenger and office keeper,	150	4,750

GOVERNMENT OF THE WESTERN TERRITORY.

The Governor for his falary as fuch, and for difcharging the duties of Superintendent of Indian affairs in the northern department,	2,000	
The Secretary of the Weftern Territory,	750	
The Three Judges, at eight hundred dollars each,	2,400	5,150

OFFICERS employed to fettle the accounts between the United States and individual States

Three Commiffioners of the General Board, at two thoufand two hundred and fifty dollars per annum,	6,750	
Chief Clerk,	600	
Four Clerks, at four hundred dollars each,	1,600	
Meffenger and office keeper,	150	
Paymafter-General, and Commiffioner of Army Accounts,	1,250	
Eight Clerks, at five hundred dollars each,	4,000	
One do at four hundred dollars,	400	
One do at four hundred and fifty dollars,	450	15,200

PENSIONS granted by the late Government

Ifaac Van Vert, John Paulding, David Williams, } a penfion of two hundred dollars per annum to each, purfuant to an act of Congrefs of 3d November, 1780,	600	
Dominique L'Eglife, per act of 8th of Auguft, 1782,	120	
Jofeph Traverfe, per do	120	
Youngeft Children of the late Major-General Warren, per act of 1ft July, 1780,	450	
Eldeft Son of do per act of 8th April, 1777, eftimated at,	600	
Youngeft Son of General Mercer, per act of 8th April, 1777, eftimated at,	700	
James M'Kenzie, Jofeph Brufiells, John Jordan, } per act of 10th September, 1783, entitled to a penfion of forty dollars each per annum,	120	
Carried forward,	2,710	242,150

ESTIMATE of MONIES Requisite for the DEPARTMENT of WAR, for the year 1790.

INFANTRY

			Dollars.
Brigadier General with the pay of Lieutenant Colonel Commandant for 12 Months at 50 Dollars,			600
2 Majors,	- - -	45	1,080
7 Captains,	- - -	35	2,940
7 Lieutenants,	- - -	30	2,520
8 Ensigns,	- - -	20	1,920
1 Paymaster,	- - - -	10	120
1 Adjutant,	- - -	10	120
1 Quarter Master,	- - -	10	120
1 Surgeon,	- - -	45	540
4 Surgeon's Mates,	- - -	30	1,440
28 Sergeants,	- - - -	6	2,016
28 Corporals,	- - - -	5	1,680
14 Musicians,	- - -	5	840
490 Privates,	- - -	4	23,520
	Carried forward,		39,456

H

Chaleston, store-keeper at 100 dols per annum,   100

     Assistant, at 15 00 per month,   - 360

Store-keeper at Philadelphia, - - - 500

Ditto, - Rhode Island, - - - 96

Ditto, - Lancaster, - - - 96

Ditto, - Fort Harkemer - - 100

His subsistence, 1 dollar per week,   52 152

   RENTS of BUILDINGS for DEPOSITS

Philadelphia, - - - 752 66

Virginia, - - - 350

West-Point, - - - 400

          ———— 1,552 66

Laboratory at the several Depost, - - 400

8 Artificers at the posts on the frontiers, including armourers,

 at 5 dollars per month, - - 480

Coopers, armourers, and carpenters employed occasionally at

 the several arsenals, - - - 500

The expence of materials and constructing twenty new carriages

 for cannon and howitzers, - - 2,000

                ————

                   7 646

      Carried forward,   - 149 666,

	Dols	Cts.	Dols.	Cts.
Brought forward,	2,710		242,150.	
Elizabeth Bergen, per act of 21st August, 1781,	53	33		
Joseph De Beauleau, per act 5th August, 1782,	100			
Richard Gridley, per acts of 17th November, 1775, and 26th February, 1781,	444	40		
Lieutenant-Colonel Touzard, per act of 27th October, 1778,	360		3,667.	73

For INCIDENTAL and CONTINGENT EXPENCES relative to the CIVIL LIST Establishment

Under this head are comprehended fire wood, stationary, together with printing work, and all other contingent expences for the two Houses of Congress, rent and office expences of the three several departments, viz. Treasury, State, War, and of the General Board of Commissioners, and Paymaster-General Congress, estimated at, — 5,000

Treasury Department, viz.

Rent,		500		
Contingencies of the Secretary's office, —		500		
	Comptroller's	400		
	Auditor's —	200		
	Register's	200		
	Treasurer's	200	2,000	
Ditto	War Department, —	600		
	Department of State,	500		
	Board of Commissioners, —	500		
	Paymaster, and Commissioner of Army Accounts, —	425	9,025	

Dollars, 254,892 73

THIS estimate corresponds with the existing provisions, but it will probably receive additions from others in the course of the session —In particular it will be observed, that there is no article respecting the salaries of Foreign Ministers, their allowances not having been regulated by law — Neither does the estimate include those objects, which remain to be provided for in consequence of some deficiency in the estimate for the services of last year, and also from certain demands on the Treasury, founded on acts of the late Government, which require an appropriation by Congress, previous to their being discharged—These will form an estimate by themselves under the head of Contingencies

Register's-Office, 5th January, 1790

JOSEPH NOURSE, Register.

[No II.]
ESTIMATE of MONIES Requisite for the DEPARTMENT of WAR, for the year 1790.
INFANTRY.

		Dollars.
1 Brigadier General with the pay of Lieutenant Colonel Commandant for 12 Months at 50 Dollars,		600
2 Majors, — — —	45	1,080
7 Captains, — —	35	2,940
7 Lieutenants, — —	30	2,520
8 Ensigns, — — —	20	1,920
1 Pay master, — — —	10	120
1 Adjutant, — —	10	120
1 Quarter Master, — — —	10	120
1 Surgeon, — — —	45	540
4 Surgeon's Mates, — —	30	1,440
28 Sergeants, — — —	6	2,016
28 Corporals, — — —	5	1,680
14 Musicians, — — —	5	840
490 Privates, — — —	4	23,520
	Carried forward,	39,456

H

	Dols	Cts.	Dols.	Cts
Brought forward, -	39.156			

ARTILLERY

1 Major 12 Months,	at 45 Dol	540		
4 Captains,	35	1,680		
8 Lieutenants,	30	2,880		
1 Surgeon's Mate,	30	360		
16 Serjeants,	6	1,152		
16 Corporals,	5	960		
4 Fifers,	5	480		
240 Matroffes,	4	11,520		
			19,572	

SUBSISTENCE

1 Brigadier General 12 Months,	at 48 Del	576		
3 Majors	20	720		
11 Captains,	12	1,584		
22 Lieutenants,	8	2,208		
1	16	192		
5 Surgeon's Mates,	8	480		
			5,760	

RATIONS

For 850 Non Commiffioned Officers and Privates, one ration pr day
count for 305 days, is 305,150 rations at 12 cents pr ration, - 36,792

			101,580	

Clothing, - 9,0 suits at 26 dollars each, - - 24,440

QUARTER MASTERS DEPARTMENT

The expence of transportation of the recruits to the frontiers,
the removal of troops from one station to another, the transportation of clothing, provifions, and military stores to the troops on the frontiers—the neceffary repairs of ordnance and other stores—the hire of teams and packhorses—the
purchase of tents, boats, axes, camp-kettles, cords, firewood, company books,
stationary for the troops, and all other expences in the quarter master's department, - - 15,000

HOSPITAL DEPARTMENT

For medicines, instruments, furniture and stores for an hospital for the frontiers,
also for attendance when neceffary at Weft-Point, - - 1,000

ORDNANCE DEPARTMENT

For salaries for the store keepers at the several depofits, viz

Weft Point, Virginia, Springfield, } 3 at 40 dollars pr month,		1,440		
Charleston, 1 Store keeper at 100 dols pr annum,	100			
2 Affistants, at 15 do pr month,	360			
1 Store keeper at Philadelphia,	500			
1 ditto, Rhode-Island,	96			
1 ditto, Lancaster,	96			
1 ditto, Fort Harkener,	120			
His subfiftence, 1 dollar pr week,	52	172		

RENTS or BUILDINGS for DEPOSITS

Philadelphia,	752 66		
Virginia,	350		
Weft Point,	400		
		1,502 66	

Labourers at the several Depofits,	400		
8 Artificers at the posts on the frontiers, including armourers, at 5 dollars pr month,	480		
Coopers, armourers, and carpenters employed occafionally at the several arsenals,	500		
The expence of materials and con tructing twenty new carriages for cannon and howitzers,	2,000		
		7,616 66	

Carried forward, - 149,606, 66

	Dol. Cts	Dols Cts.
Brought forward,	-	149,666 66

Buildings for arsenals and magazines are highly requisite in the southern and middle departments, for which particularly estimates will be formed

CONTINGENCIES of the WAR Department, viz

For maps, hiring expresses, allowance to officers for extra expences, printing, loss of stores of all kinds, advertising and apprehending deserters, | - | - | 3,000

CONTINGENCIES of the WAR Office, viz

Office rent, wood, stationary, desks, book cases, sweeping, &c		600
Subsistence due the officers of Colonel Marinus Willet's regiment in 1782,	786 6	
Pay due Lieutenant Joseph Wilson, pay master to the regiment lately commanded by Col David Humphreys,	315	
Pay subsistence and forage due the officers appointed by the State of Rhode-Island, under the act of Congress of the 20th October, 1786,	1,770	2,871 6

		156,177 72

Total amount as above, - - 156,137 72
Deduct contingencies of the War Office, office rent, wood, stationary, desks, &c is 1000, the same being included with the advance to the civil list compute, - - 600

	Dollars 155,537 72

Summary of the foregoing,	
Pay of the troops,	59,028
Subsistence do.	12,557
Clothing of ditto,	21,040
Quarter masters department,	15,000
Hospital department,	1,000
Contingencies of the war department,	3,000
Contingencies of the war office,	600
Arrears of pay and subsistence unprovided for,	28,716
Ordnance department,	7,640 00

War Office, December 29th, 1789

Dollars, 155,537 72

(Signed) HENRY KNOX Secretary for the Department of War

[A, No. III]

ESTIMATE of the Annual PENSIONS of the INVALIDS of the United States, taken from returns in the War-Office, dated as follows

			Dol. Cts	Dol. Cts
November 28, 1789,	-	New Hampshire,	3,000	
December 1,	-	Massachusetts,	11,166	
December 1,	-	Connecticut,	7,200	
December 31,	-	Maryland,	15,538	
January 2,	-	New-York,	4,957 6	
December 12,	-	Pennsylvania,	16,556	
June 1787,	-	Virginia,	9,276 66	
				67,713 72

Original fund—No returns having been received

from the Rhode-Island and Delaware nearly equal to New-Hampshire, 3,172
And ordnance accounts Connecticut, 7,200
North-Carolina, South-Carolina and Georgia, with regard to New-Jersey, Connecticut and Virginia, 19,591

	29,766

	Dollars, 96,979 72

(Signed) H KNOX, Secretary for the Department of War

War Office, 31st December, 1789

For Schedule K, which should have been inserted here, see the last page

An ACT repealing, after the laſt day of   next, the Duties heretofore laid upon diſtilled Spirits imported from abroad, and laying others in their ſtead, and alſo upon Spirits diſtilled within the United States, as well to diſcourage the exceſſive uſe of thoſe Spirits, and promote Agriculture, as to provide for the ſupport of the Public Credit, and for the Common Defence and General Welfare

I   **B**E it enacted by the Senate and Houſe of Repreſentatives of the United States of America in Congreſs aſſembled,* that after the laſt day of   next, the duties laid on diſtilled ſpirits by the act entitled " An act for laying a duty on goods, wares and merchandizes imported into the United States," ſhall ceaſe ; and that upon all diſtilled ſpirits which ſhall be imported into the United States, after that day, from any foreign port or place, there ſhall be paid for their uſe the duties following, that is to ſay,

1ſt   For every gallon of thoſe ſpirits more than ten per cent. below proof, according to Dicas's hydrometer, twenty cents

2d   For every gallon of thoſe ſpirits under five, and not more than ten per cent below proof, according to the ſame hydrometer, twenty-one cents

3d   For every gallon of thoſe ſpirits of proof, and not more than five per cent below proof according to the ſame hydrometer, twenty-two cents

4th   For every gallon of thoſe ſpirits above proof, but not exceeding twenty per cent according to the ſame hydrometer, twenty-five cents

5th   For every gallon of thoſe ſpirits more than twenty, and not more than forty per cent above proof, according to the ſame hydrometer, thirty cents

6th   For every gallon of thoſe ſpirits, more than forty per cent above proof, according to the ſame hydrometer, forty cents

II   And be it further enacted, that the ſaid duties ſhall be collected in the ſame manner, by the ſame perſons, under the ſame regulations, and ſubject to the ſame forfeitures and other penalties, as thoſe heretofore laid ; the act concerning which ſhall be deemed to be in full force for the collection of the duties herein before impoſed, except as to the alterations contained in this act

III   And be it further enacted,† that the ſaid duties, at the option of the proprietor, importer or conſignee, may either be paid immediately, or ſecured by bond, with one or more ſureties, to the ſatisfaction of the collector, or perſon acting as ſuch, with condition for the payment of one moiety in four months, and the other moiety in eight months   Provided that where the ſaid duties ſhall not exceed fifty dollars, the ſame ſhall be immediately paid ; and that where the ſame ſhall exceed fifty dollars, if the ſaid proprietor, importer or conſignee ſhall think fit to make preſent payment thereof, there ſhall be an abatement to him or her, at the rate of ſeven per cent per annum, only for ſuch preſent payment, the allowance of ten per cent in the ſaid former act notwithſtanding

And as not only a due regard to the exigencies of the public, and to the intereſt and eaſe of the community, but juſtice to thoſe virtuous citizens, who, content with the emoluments of fair and honorable trade, diſdain to violate the laws of their country, and the principles of probity, requires that every poſſible impediment ſhould be oppoſed to the fraudulent views of thoſe who wiſh to profit at the expence both of the fair trader and of the community——

IV   Be it further enacted,‡ that the Preſident of the United States of America, be authoriſed to appoint, with the advice and conſent of the Senate, ſuch number of officers as ſhall appear to him neceſſary, to be denominated Inſpectors of the revenue ; and to aſſign to them reſpectively ſuch diſtricts or limits for the exerciſe of their reſpective offices, as he ſhall judge beſt adapted to the due execution thereof ; dividing the diſtricts, if he ſhall think it adviſeable, into general and particular, and placing the Inſpectors of the latter under the ſuperintendance of the former, within the limits whereof they ſhall be reſpectively comprehended ; and alſo to make ſuch allowances to the ſaid Inſpectors, and to the Deputies and officers by them appointed and employed for their reſpective ſervices in the execution of this act, to be paid out of the product of the ſaid duties, as ſhall be reaſon

* *The four firſt of theſe claſſes of proof correſpond with the different kinds of ſpirits now uſually imported The firſt with gin, the ſecond with St. Croix rum, the third with Antigua rum, the fourth with Jamaica ſpirit, the fifth correſponds with the uſual proof of high wines, the laſt with that of Alcohol Theſe diſtinctions are neceſſary, not only to proportion the duty, but to prevent evaſions of it According to the preſent act, high wines, or even Alcohol, which is from 30 to 40 per cent above Jamaica proof, might be imported liable only to the duty of Jamaica proof*

† *The extenſion of the time is for the accommodation of the merchants in conſideration of the encreaſed rate.—It is propoſed to reduce the diſcount, becauſe ten per cent is more than either the intereſt of money, or the riſk of non-payment ſeems to warrant. Generally ſpeaking, tranſient perſons are thoſe who avail themſelves of the advantage, and they, without it, would commonly pay down, from the inconvenience of procuring and leaving ſureties*

‡ *This appears to be the only practicable method of compaſſing the details of ſo complicated a buſineſs.*

able and proper Provided always, that the whole amount of the said allowances shall not exceed
per cent of the said product, computed throughout the United States, and that, being
once regulated by the said President, they shall be alterable in such manner only as shall from time
to time be prescribed by law

V. And be it further enacted, that the Inspector or Inspectors of the revenue for each district,
shall establish one or more offices within the same, and that there shall be one at least at each port
of delivery, and in order that the said offices may be publicly known, there shall be painted or
written, in large legible characters, upon some conspicuous part outside and in front of each house
building or place in which any such office shall be kept, these words, ' Office of Inspection ' and
if any person shall paint or write, or cause to be painted or written, the said words, upon any other
than such house or building, he or she shall forfeit and pay for so doing, one hundred dollars

VI. And be it further enacted, that within forty-eight hours after any ship or vessel, having on
board any distilled Spirits brought in such ship or vessel from any foreign port or place, shall arrive within any port of the United States, whether the same be the first port of arrival of such ship
or vessel or not, the master or person having the command or charge thereof, shall report to the
Inspector or other chief officer of Inspection of the port to which she shall to arrive, the place from
which she last sailed with her name and burthen and the quantity and kinds of the said spirits on
board of her, and the casks or cases containing them, with their marks and numbers on pain of forfeiting five hundred dollars

VII. And be it further enacted, that the Collector or other officer acting as Collector or
of any port, with whom entry shall have been made of any of the said spirits, performing to be forfeiting a duty on goods, wares and merchandize imported into the United States, shall forthwith after such entry certify and transmit the same, as particularly as it shall have been made with
him, to the Inspector of the revenue, or other proper officer of inspection, of the port where it shall
be intended to commence the delivery of the spirits so entered or any part thereof, for which purpose, every proprietor, importer or consignee, making entry as aforesaid shall deliver a memoran-
dum or certificate, upon oath or affirmation, which the said certificate shall specify and declare the true intent thereof, and
the port at which the said delivery shall be intended to be commenced, to the Collector or officer
with whom the same shall be made And every person permitted by such Collector to make entry
of any of the said spirits, shall previous to such landing have produced to the said officer or officers
who shall take a memorandum proper to be kept of the same, and shall in consideration of
the word " Inspected," the time to land, and his own name, after which he shall return it to the
person by whom it shall have been produced, and then, and not otherwise, it shall be lawful to
land the spirits therein specified, and if the said spirits shall be removed without such certificate
upon the same for that purpose, the master or person having charge of the ship or vessel
from which the same shall have been landed, shall for every such offence forfeit the sum of five
hundred dollars

VIII. And be it further enacted, That whenever it shall be intended that any ship or vessel shall
proceed with the whole or any part of the spirits which shall have been brought in such ship or vessel from any foreign port or place, from one port in the United States to another port in the said
United States, which in the first case of such spirits, the master or person having the command or charge of such ship or vessel, shall previous to her departure apply to the proper officer
of inspection for the port from which she is about to depart, for a certificate of the quantity and
particulars of such of the said spirits as shall have been certified or reported to have been entered or imported in such ship or vessel, and of the particulars thereof shall appear to him to have been and part-
of her at such port, which certificate the said officer shall deliver, with great care and to be on charge.
And the master or person having the command or charge of such ship or vessel, shall, within twenty-four hours after her arrival at the port to which the delivery is made, deliver the said certificate
to the proper officer of inspection of such last mentioned port And if such ship or vessel shall proceed from one port to another within the United States, with the whole or any part of the spirits
brought in her, and provided with the same as obtained such certificate, or if within twenty four
hours after her arrival at such other port, the said certificate shall not be delivered to the proper officer of inspection there, the master or person having the command or charge of the said ship or
vessel, shall in each case incur a forfeiture, as if the whole cargo of no other such had
arrival, shall be forfeited, and may be seized by any officer of inspection

IX. And be it further enacted, That all spirits which shall be imported as aforesaid, shall be
landed under the inspection of the officer or officers of inspection for the place where the same shall
be landed, and not otherwise, on pain of forfeiture thereof for which purpose the said officer or
officers shall at all reasonable times attend Provided that this shall not be construed to exclude the
inspection of the officers of the customs as now established and practised

X. And be it further enacted, That the officers of inspection, under whose survey any of the
said spirits shall be landed, shall, upon landing thereof, and as soon as the casks and cases containing the same shall be gauged or measured, brand or otherwise mark in durable characters, the se-

I

veral casks or cases containing the same, with progressive numbers, and also with the name of the ship or vessel wherein the same was or were imported, and of the port of entry, and with the proof and quantity thereof, together with such other marks if any other shall be deemed needful, as the respective inspectors of the revenue may direct. And the said officer shall keep a book, wherein he shall enter the name of each vessel in which any of the said spirits shall be so imported, and of the port of entry and of delivery, and of the master of such vessel, and of each importer, and the several casks and cases containing the same, and the marks of each, and if not an inspector or the chief officer of inspection for the place, shall as soon as may be thereafter, make an exact transcript of each entry, and deliver the same to such inspector or chief officer, who shall keep a like book for recording the said transcripts.

XI. And be it further enacted, That the inspector of the revenue or other chief officer of inspection within whose survey any of the said spirits shall be landed shall give to the proprietor, importer, or consignee thereof, or his or her agent, a certificate to remain with him or her of the whole quantity of the said spirits which shall have been so landed, which certificate besides the said quantity shall specify the name of such proprietor, importer, or consignee, and of the vessel from on board which the said spirits shall have been landed, and of the marks of each cask or case containing the same. And the said inspector or other chief officer of inspection shall deliver to the said proprietor, importer or consignee, or to his or her agent, a like certificate for each cask or case which shall accompany the same wheresoever it shall be sent as evidence of its being lawfully imported. And the officer of inspection granting the said certificates, shall make regular and exact entries in the book to be by him kept as aforesaid, of all spirits for which the same shall be granted as particularly as therein described. And the said proprietor, importer, or consignee, or his or her agent upon the sale and delivery of any of the said spirits, shall deliver to the purchaser or purchasers thereof, the certificate or certificates which ought to accompany the same, on pain of forfeiting the sum of fifty dollars for each cask or case with which such certificate shall not be delivered.

XII. And be it further enacted,* That upon all spirits which after the said last day of   next, shall be distilled within the United States, wholly or in part from molasses, sugar, or other foreign materials, there shall be paid for their use the duties following, that is to say—

1st For every gallon of those spirits more than 10 per cent below proof, according to Dica's hydrometer, eleven cents

2d For every gallon of those spirits under five and not more than ten per cent below proof, according to the same hydrometer, twelve cents

3d For every gallon of those spirits of proof, and not more than five per cent below proof, according to the same hydrometer, thirteen cents

4th For every gallon of those spirits above proof, and not exceeding twenty per cent according to the same hydrometer, fifteen cents

5th For every gallon of those spirits more than twenty and not more than forty per cent above proof, according to the said hydrometer, twenty cents

6th For every gallon of those spirits more than forty per cent above proof, according to the same hydrometer, thirty cents.

XIII And be it further enacted,† That upon all spirits which after the said last day of   next, shall be distilled within the United States, from any article of the growth or production of the United States, in any city, town or village, there shall be paid for their use the duties following, that is to say —

1st For every gallon of those spirits more than ten per cent below proof, according to Dicas's hydrometer, nine cents

2d For every gallon of those spirits under five and not more than ten per cent below proof, according to the same hydrometer, ten cents

3d For every gallon of those spirits of proof, and not more than five per cent below proof, according to the same hydrometer, eleven cents

4th For every gallon of those spirits above proof, but not exceeding twenty per cent according to the same hydrometer, thirteen cents

* The first class of proof here corresponds with what is understood by common proof at our distilleries and answers to that of gin. Hence our common rum, compared with the lowest kind of imported rum, and including the duty on molasses, stands charged in the proportion of 14 to 21, which difference it is presumed will afford due encouragement. The remaining classes also correspond with those above.

† The several classes of proof here agree with those in the preceding section, but it will be observed that the rates are lower. This will operate as an encouragement to distillation from our own materials. It is evident that a higher duty being laid on spirits distilled from foreign materials, than on those made from our own, the difference is a bounty on the latter, and places it in a better situation than if there were no duty on either; in general it may be remarked, that the rates proposed on these different kinds of spirits, though considerably higher than heretofore, are much less than they bear in most other countries.

5th For every gallon of thofe fpirits more than twenty and not more than forty per cent. above proof, according to the fame hydrometer, feventeen cents

6 For every gallon of thofe fpirits more than forty per cent above proof, according to the fame hydrometer, twenty-five cents

XIV And be it further enacted, That the faid duties on fpirits diftilled within the United States, fhall be collected under the management of the infpectors of the revenue

XV And be it further enacted, That the faid duties on fpirits diftilled within the United States, fhall be paid or fecured previous to the removal thereof from the diftilleries at which they are refpectively made And it fhall be at the option of the proprietor or proprietors of each diftillery, or of his, her or their agent having the fuperintendence thereof, either to pay the faid duties previous to fuch removal, with an abatement at the rate of two cents for every ten gallons, or to fecure the payment of the fame, by giving bond quarter yearly, with one or more fureties, to the fatisfaction of the officer of infpection within whofe furvey fuch diftillery fhall be, and in fuch fum as the faid officer fhall direct, with condition for the obfervance of the regulations in this act contained, on his, her, or their part, and alfo for the payment of the duties upon all fuch of the faid fpirits as fhall be removed from fuch diftillery, within three months next enfuing the date of the bond, at the expiration of fix months from the faid date

XVI And be it further enacted * That the infpector or infpectors of each diftrict, fhall appoint a proper officer to have the charge and furvey of each diftillery within his or their diftrict, who fhall attend fuch diftillery at all reafonable times, for the execution of the duties by this act enjoined upon him

XVII And be it further enacted, That previous to the removal of any of the faid fpirits from any diftillery, the officer of infpection within whofe furvey the fame may be, fhall brand or otherwife mark each cafk containing the fame in durable characters, and with progreffive numbers, and with the name of the acting owner or other manager of fuch diftillery, and of the place where the fame was fituate, and with the quantity therein, to be afcertained by actual gauging, and with the amount thereof And the duties thereupon having been firft paid, or fecured, as above provided, the faid officer fhall grant a certificate for each cafk of the faid fpirits, to accompany the fame wherefoever it fhall be fent, purporting that the duty thereupon hath been paid or fecured as the cafe may be, and defcribing each cafk by its marks, and fhall enter in a book for that purpofe to be kept, all the fpirits diftilled at fuch diftillery, and removed from the fame, and the marks of each cafk, and the perfons for whofe ufe, and the places to which removed, and the time of each removal, and the amount of the duties on the fpirits fo removed And if any certified fpirit fhall be removed from any fuch diftillery without having been branded or marked as aforefaid, or without fuch certificate as aforefaid, the fame, together with the cafk or cafks containing them, and the horfes and wagons, with their harnefs and tackling, employed in removing them, fhall be forfeited, and may be feized by any officer of infpection And the fuperintendent or manager of fuch diftillery fhall alfo forfeit the full value of the fpirits fo removed, to be computed at the higheft price of the like fpirits in the market

XVIII And be it further enacted, That no fpirits fhall be removed from any fuch diftillery except by a perfon or perfons licenfed in the manner herein after directed, nor at any other times than between the hour of   and the hour of
                                          and between the hour of
                                          and the hour of   of
each day, from the   day of
to the   day of   in
each year , and between the hour of
                                          and the hour of   and
between the hour of   and the
hour of   of each day, from
the   day of   to the
                            day of   in each year

XIX And be it further enacted, †That licenfes to convey or carry fpirits from the faid diftilleries, fhall, in each diftrict, be granted by the infpector or infpectors of the revenue thereof, to fuch diftrict perfon or perfons as fhall appear to him or them proper for the truft, who fhall refpectively

---

* This infpection is effential to a fecure collection Experience has fhewn that proper dependence cannot be placed on any plan which relies on the exactnefs of the accounts to be rendered by the individuals interefted, and fuch a reliance not only affects the revenue, but throws an undue proportion of the burthen on the upright and confcientious

† This regulation would certainly add much to the fafety of the collection But it is doubtful whether it would not be exceptionable in fome parts of the country Perhaps it may be limited to the principal cities or it may be general, and a difcretion vefted fomewhere, to make the neceffary exceptions

give bonds, with one or more sureties to the satisfaction of the said inspector or inspectors of the revenue, in a sum not exceeding   dollars, nor less than   dollars, with condition faithfully and diligently, to carry and deliver all such of the said spirits as shall be committed to their care respectively, and in so doing to observe the directions of this act Provided always, That nothing herein contained shall in any wise infringe or interfere with any exclusive privilege which any individuals or bodies politic may have or be entitled to, by virtue of any charter, grant or act of incorporation touching the right of carrying or of licensing persons to carry goods and commodities within particular limits But where any such privilege shall exist, the persons to be licensed pursuant to this act, shall execute the trust thereby reposed in them, through and by means of the person or persons who by virtue of such privilege shall be authorised to carry within such limits, and in such manner as shall be perfectly consistent with such privilege and not otherwise

XX And be it further enacted,† That upon stills which after the 1st day of   next, shall be employed in distilling spirits from materials of the growth or production of the United States, in any other place than a city, town or village, there shall be paid for the use of the United States, the yearly duty of sixty cents for every gallon, English wine measure, of the capacity or content of each and every such still, including the head thereof Provided that the said duty shall not extend to any still of less than   except where such still shall be worked at the same distillery, together with another of dimensions exceeding   gallons

XXI And be it further enacted, That the evidence of the employment of the said stills shall be, their being erected in stone, brick or some other manner whereby they shall be in a condition to be worked

XXII And be it further enacted, That the said duties on stills shall be collected under the management of the inspectors of the revenue, who in each district shall appoint and assign proper officers for the surveys of the said stills, and the admeasurement thereof, and the collection of the duties thereupon, and the said duties shall be paid half yearly, within the first fifteen days of the months of   and   upon demand made of the proprietor or proprietors of each still at his, her or their dwelling, by the proper officer charged with the survey thereof And in case of refusal or neglect to pay, the amount of the duties so refused or neglected to be paid, may either be recovered with costs of suit in an action of debt in the name of the inspector or inspectors of the district, with which such refusal shall happen, or may be levied by distress and sale of goods of the person or persons refusing or neglecting to pay, rendering the overplus (if any there be after payment of the said amount and the charges of distress and sale) to the said person or persons.

And whereas the duties hereby charged upon stills, have been estimated upon a computation that a still of each of the dimensions herein before enumerated, worked for the usual time would produce in the course of a year a quantity of spirits, which at the rate of   cents per gallon, would amount to the duty charged thereon And as from different causes it may in some instances happen, that the said computation   the said stills to greater duties than are intended,

XXIII Be it therefore enacted, That if the proprietor of any such still finding himself or herself aggrieved by the said rates, shall enter or cause to be entered in a book or on a paper to be kept for that purpose, from day to day when such still shall be employed the quantity of spirits distilled therefrom, and the quantity from time to time sold or otherwise disposed of, and to whom and when, and shall produce   the present officer of inspection   shall be   upon oath, that known   affirmation, th   doth contain to the best   knowledge and belief, true entries   of their of,   dates of all the spirits distilled therefrom   to   shall   from such still, and of the disposition thereof,   that   upon oath or affirmation the quantity of such spirits then remaining on hand, it shall be lawful in   for the said officer to whom the said book or paper shall be produced, and   such still, according to the quantity so stated to   made therefrom at the rate   per gallon, which, and no more, shall be   the same Provided, That if the said entries be made by any person other than the said proprietor, a like oath or affirmation shall be made by such person

---

† The duty is here laid upon the stills because it would be inconvenient, to extend the inspection of the officers in its full extent throughout the country The rates is adjusted according to an estimate of what a still of any given dimensions, worked for the usual time is capable of producing, but lest this rule should in any instance operate injuriously, it is by a subsequent provision put in the power of the proprietor to redress himself This provision certainly opens a door to fraud, but it is presumed to be adviseable to submit to this inconvenience rather than to those which would be apt to attend the supposition of inequality

And the more effectually to prevent the evasion of the duties hereby imposed to the no less injury of the trader than of the revenue,

XXIV. Be it further enacted, *That every person who shall be a dealer or trader in distilled spirits (except as a maker or distiller thereof) in the original casks or cases in which they shall be imported, or in quantities of twenty five gallons at one sale, shall be deemed a wholesale dealer in spirits, and shall write or paint or cause to be written or painted, in large, legible and durable characters, upon some conspicuous part outside and in front of each house or other building or place, and upon the door or usual entrance of each vault, cellar or apartment within the same in which any of the said spirits shall be at any time by him or her deposited or kept or intended to to be, the words " wholesale dealer in spirits," and shall also, within three days at least before he or she shall begin to keep or sell any of the said spirits therein make a particular entry in writing at the nearest office of inspection of the district in which the same shall be situate, if within ten miles thereof of every such house or other building or place, and of each cellar, vault, or apartment within the same in which he or she shall intend to put or keep any of the said spirits, and if any such dealer shall omit to write or paint, or cause to be written or painted the words aforesaid, and in manner aforesaid, upon any such house or other building or place, or vault, cellar or apartment thereof, in which he or she shall so have or keep any of the said spirits, or shall in case the same be situated within the said distance of ten miles of any office of inspection omit to make entry thereof as aforesaid, such dealer shall for every such omission or neglect forfeit the sum of five hundred dollars, and all the spirits which he or she shall have or keep therein, or the value thereof to be computed at the highest price of such spirits in the market

XXV. And be it further enacted, That every person who shall be a maker or distiller of spirits shall write or paint or cause to be written or painted upon some conspicuous part outside and in front of each house or other building or place made use of or intended to be made use of by him or her for the distillation or keeping of spirituous liquors, and upon the door or usual entrance of each vault, cellar or apartment within the same in which any of the said liquors shall be at any time by him or her distilled, deposited or kept, or intended to to be, the words " Distiller of spirits," and shall also, three days at least before he or she shall begin to distil therein, make a particular entry in writing, at the nearest office of inspection, if within ten miles thereof, of every such house, building or place, and of each vault, cellar and apartment within the same, in which he or she shall intend to carry on the business of distilling, or to keep any spirits by him or her distilled. And if any such distiller shall omit to paint or write, or cause to be painted or written the words aforesaid, in manner aforesaid, upon any such house or other building or place, or vault, cellar or apartment thereof, or shall, in case the same be situate within the said distance of ten miles or any office of inspection, omit to make entry thereof as aforesaid, such distiller shall for every such omission or neglect, forfeit the sum of five hundred dollars, and all the spirits which he or she shall have or keep therein, or the value thereof, to be computed at the highest price of such spirits in the market: Provided also, and be it further enacted, that the said entry to be made by persons who shall be dealers in or distillers of spirits on the last day of   next, shall be made on that day, or within three days thereafter, accompanied (except where the duties hereby imposed are charged on the still) with a true and particular account or inventory of the spirits, on that day and at the time, in every or any house, building or place by him or her entered, and of the casks, cases and vessels containing the same, with their marks and numbers, and the quantities and qualities of the spirits therein contained, on pain of forfeiting, for neglecting to make such entry, or to deliver such account, the sum of five hundred dollars, and all the spirits by him or her had or kept in any such house, building or place. And provided further, that nothing herein contained shall be construed to exempt any such distiller, who shall be, besides his dealing as a distiller, a dealer or trader in distilled spirits as described in the twenty-fourth section of this act, from the regulations therein pre-

---

* The provisions in this section form an essential part of the plan. They serve to bring all those who deal in the sale of spirits in considerable quantities, and the places in which they are kept, under the immediate eye of the law. It must always be very difficult to conceal any quantity of spirits in a place which is not announced and entered in the manner prescribed. Whoever sees them in any such place, or in going from it, will know that they are liable to forfeiture, and will have inducements enough to give intelligence of the fact. And when every man can, from so simple a circumstance, discern that a fraud has been committed, it will be hardly possible for it to escape detection. Besides this, the article, whenever it leaves its concealment, is liable to discovery from the want of those indications which are necessary to shew that it was lawfully imported or made. And it is not supposeable that it can continue concealed, and pass safe through all its stages, from the importation or making, to the consumption. The consumer himself, if not interested in the fraud, will detect and disclose it. The necessity of entry is limited to a distance of ten miles, to prevent inconvenience ——In remote places, where little business is done, the precaution may be relaxed, and offices of inspection will be found less necessary. Articles must be carried, for sale, to places where there is considerable demand, and if at such places the requisite guards are kept up with strictness, the end will be substantially answered.

K

scribed but every such distiller, so being also a dealer or trader in distilled spirits, shall observe and shall be subject to all the rules, regulations and penalties herein specified

XXVI. And be it further enacted, that where any entry shall be made by any such dealer, of any such house, building or other place for keeping of any of the said spirits, no other such dealer, not being in partnership with the dealer aforesaid, making such entry, shall on any pretence make entry of the same house or building, or of any apartment, vault, cellar or place within the same house, building or tenement in which such first entry shall then be existing; but every such other dealer, making such further entry of the same house, building or place, or of any apartment, vault, cellar or place within the same, shall, notwithstanding such further entry, be deemed a dealer without entry, and shall be subject to the like penalties and forfeitures as any dealers without entry are subject to by this act.

XXVII. And be it further enacted, that the Inspector or Inspectors of the revenue for the district wherein any house, building or place shall be situate, whereof entry shall be made as last aforesaid, shall as soon as may be thereafter, visit and inspect, or cause to be visited and inspected by some proper officer or officers of inspection, every such house or other building or place within his or their district, and shall take or cause to be taken an exact account of the spirits therein respectively contained, and shall mark or cause to be marked in durable characters, the several casks, cases or vessels containing the same, with progressive numbers, and allow with the name or each dealer or distiller to whom the same may belong, or in whose custody the same may be, and the quantities, kinds and proofs of spirits therein contained, and these words, " Old Stock." And the said inspector or inspectors shall keep a book wherein he or they shall enter the name of every such dealer or distiller within his or their district, and the particulars of such old stock in the possession of each, designating the several casks and cases containing the same, and their respective quantities, kinds, proofs and marks. And he or they shall also give a certificate to every such dealer or distiller, of the quantity and particulars of such old stock in his or her possession, and a separate certificate for each cask, case or vessel, describing the same, according to its marks, which certificate shall accompany the same wheresoever it shall be sent. And in case there shall be no officer of inspection within the said distance of ten miles of any such house or other building or place, then it shall be the duty of such dealer to whom the same may belong, to mark with the like durable characters the several casks containing the spirits therein, and in like manner as above directed to be done by the said Inspector or Inspectors. And the said dealer shall make entry thereof in some proper book or in some proper paper to be by him or her kept for that purpose, specifying particularly each cask, case or vessel, and its marks, and the quantity and quality of the spirits therein contained (of which entry he or she shall, upon request, deliver an exact copy to the Inspector or Inspectors of the revenue for the district) and if required by him or them, shall attest the same by oath, or, being a known Quaker by affirmation. And the said dealer, with every such cask, case or vessel which shall be delivered out of his or her house or other building or place, shall give a certificate or permit, signed by himself or herself, of the like import of that above directed to be given by the said Inspector or Inspectors, which certificate shall in like manner accompany the same wheresoever it may be sent. And if any such dealer shall in the said case omit to mark the said several casks, cases or vessels containing the said spirits, or to make entry thereof in some proper book, or on some proper paper as aforesaid, he or she shall forfeit and pay for every such neglect two hundred dollars. And if in the same case he or she shall deliver out or send away any of the said spirits without such certificate by him or her directed to be furnished as aforesaid, the said spirits so delivered out or sent away, shall be forfeited, and may be seized by any officer of inspection, and the said dealer shall also forfeit the full value thereof.

XXVIII. And be it further enacted, that every proprietor of any still on which a duty shall be charged according to the twentieth section of this act, shall brand or otherwise mark in durable characters, every cask, barrel or keg containing any spirit distilled by him or her, previous to the sale thereof, with his or her name, and with progressive numbers, and shall grant a certificate with each cask, barrel or keg by him or her sold, describing the same by its marks, and purporting that the same was made by him or her, to accompany such cask, barrel or keg, wheresoever it shall be sent.

XXIX. And be it further enacted, that when any such wholesale dealer in spirits, shall bring in his or her entered house, building or place, any of the said spirits, if such house, building or place be within two miles of any office of inspection, he or she shall within twenty-four hours after the said spirits shall be brought into such house, building or place, send notice thereof in writing to the said office, specifying therein the quantity and kinds of the spirits so brought in, and the marks of the cask or casks, case or cases containing the same, on pain of forfeiting, for every neglect to give such notice, fifty dollars. And it shall be the duty of the officer to whom such notice shall be given, forthwith thereafter to inspect and take an account of such spirits.

XXX. And be it further enacted, that if any distilled spirits shall be found in the possession of any such dealer, without the proper certificates which ought to accompany the same, it shall be presumptive evidence that the same are liable to forfeiture, and it shall be lawful for any officer of inspection to seize them as forfeited; and if, upon the trial in consequence of such seizure, the owner or claimant of the spirits seized, shall not prove that the same were imported into the United States according to law, or were distilled as mentioned in the twelfth and thirteenth sections of this act, and the duties thereupon paid, or were distilled at one of the stills mentioned in the twentieth section of this act, they shall be adjudged to be forfeited.

XXXI   And be it further enacted, that it shall be lawful for the officers of inspection of each district, at all times in the day time, upon request, to enter into all and every the houses, store-houses, ware-houses, buildings and places, which shall have been entered by the said wholesale dealers in manner aforesaid, and by tasting, guaging or otherwise to take an account of the quantity, kinds and proofs of the said spirits therein contained, and also to take samples thereof, paying for the same the usual price

XXXII   And be it further enacted, that every such dealer shall keep the several kinds of spirits in his or her entered warehouse, building or place, separate and apart from each other, on pain of forfeiting upon every conviction of neglect one hundred dollars; and shall also, upon request, shew to the officers of inspection of the district wherein he or she is so a dealer, or to any of them, each and every cask, vessel and case in which he or she shall keep any distilled spirits, and the certificates which ought to accompany the same, upon pain of forfeiting every such cask, vessel or case, as shall be shewn, together with the spirits therein contained

XXXIII   And be it further enacted, that if any person or persons shall rub out or deface any of the marks set upon any cask or case pursuant to the directions of this act, such person or persons shall, for every such offence, forfeit and pay the sum of one hundred dollars

XXXIV   And be it further enacted, that no cask, barrel, keg, vessel or case, marked as " Old stock," shall be made use of by any dealer or distiller of spirits, for putting or keeping therein any spirits other than those which were contained therein when so marked, on pain of forfeiting five hundred dollars for every cask, barrel, keg, vessel or case wherein any such other spirits shall be so put or kept   Neither shall any such dealer have or keep any distilled spirits in any such cask, barrel, keg, vessel or case, longer than for the space of one year from the said last day of   next, on pain of forfeiting the said spirits

XXXV   And be it further enacted, that in case any of the said spirits shall be fraudulently deposited, hid or concealed in any place whatsoever, with intent to evade the duties hereby imposed upon them, they shall be forfeited   And for the better discovery of any such spirits so fraudulently deposited, hid or concealed, it shall be lawful for any Inspector of the revenue, or for any Judge of any Court of the United States, or either of them, or for any Justice of the peace, upon reasonable cause of suspicion, to be made out to the satisfaction of such Inspector, Judge or Justice, by the oath, or, in the case of a known Quaker, by the affirmation, of any person or persons, by special warrant or warrants under their respective hands and seals, to authorise any of the officers of inspection, by day or night, but if in the night time in the presence of a constable or other officer of the peace, to enter into all and every such place and places, in which any of the said spirits shall be suspected to be so fraudulently deposited, hid or concealed, and to seize and carry away any of the said spirits which shall be there found, so fraudulently deposited, hid or concealed, as forfeited

XXXVI   And be it further enacted, That no person shall carry on the business of distilling, rectifying or compounding of spirituous liquors in any cellar, vault, or other place below the surface of the ground, or have or use any pipes, stop cocks, or other communications under ground, for the purpose of conveying spirituous liquors from one back or vessel to another, or from any such back or vessel to its still, or to any other place, on pain of forfeiting for every such place, below the surface of the ground in which the said business shall be carried on the sum of five hundred dollars, and for every such pipe, stop-cock, or other communication under ground, the sum of two hundred and fifty dollars   And in case the said person shall carry on the said business in any such place below the surface of the ground, or shall have or use any such communication under ground, it shall be lawful for any inspector of the revenue, or Judge of any court of the United States, or Judge of any court of a particular State, or Justice of the Peace, upon reasonable cause of suspicion to be made out to the satisfaction of such inspector, judge or justice, by oath or affirmation of any person or persons, by special warrant under his or either of their respective hands and seals, to authorise any of the officers of inspection, by day or night, but if in the night, in the presence of a constable or other officer of the peace, to enter into all and every such place or places after request first made, and the cause declared, therein to search and examine for the same, and for that purpose to break the ground, wall, partition or other place, and upon finding such cellar, vault, or other building, or place below the surface of the ground, or such pipe, stop-cock, or other communication under ground, to destroy the same, and to seize such spirituous liquors as may be found below the surface of the ground, or which shall have been conveyed through such pipe, stop-cock, or other communication, which warrant or warrants may be lawfully executed by such officer accordingly   Provided that nothing herein contained shall be construed to authorise any inspector of the revenue to issue any warrant to himself, or upon

his own oath, to any other officer. And provided farther, That if upon such search, no place below
the surface of the ground, nor any such pipe, stop-cock, or other communication be found, the said
officer shall make good the ground, wall, partition, or other place so broken up as aforesaid, together with such reasonable damages as shall be adjudged by two neighboring justices of the peace on
the party or parties injured pursuing his, her or their action against such officer of inspection, for
the damages so sustained, which damages in either case, shall be paid out of the revenue arising
from the act.

XXXVII. And be it further enacted, * That after the last day of   next, no spirituous
liquors, except gin in cases, shall be brought from any foreign port or place in any other way than
in casks capable each of containing one hundred gallons at the least, on pain of forfeiture of the
said spirits, and of the ship or vessel in which they shall be brought. Provided always, That nothing in this act contained, shall be construed to forfeit any spirits for being imported or brought
into the United States, in other casks or vessels than as aforesaid, or the ship or vessel in which they
shall be brought, if such spirits shall be for the use of the seamen on board such ship or vessel, and
shall not exceed the quantity of   gallons for each such seaman.

XXXVIII. And be it further enacted, That in every case in which any of the said spirits shall be
forfeited by virtue of this act, the casks, vessels and cases containing the same, shall also be forfeited.

XXXIX. And be it further enacted, That every dealer by wholesale, or distiller of spirits, on which
the duty is hereby charged by the gallon, shall keep or cause to be kept, an exact account of all the
said spirits which he or she shall sell, send out or distill, distinguishing their several kinds and proofs,
and shall every day make a just and true entry in a book or on a paper, to be kept for that purpose,
of the quantities and particulars of the said spirits by him or her sold, sent out or distilled, on the preceding day, specifying the marks of the several casks in which they shall be so sold or sent out, and
the persons to whom, and for whose use they shall be so sold or sent out. Which said books and papers
shall be prepared for the making such entries and shall be delivered upon demand to the said dealers
and distillers by the inspectors of the revenue of the several districts, or by such person or persons
as they shall respectively for that purpose appoint, and shall be severally returned or delivered at the
end of each year, or when the same shall be respectively filled up, which shall first happen to the
proper officers of inspection, and the truth of the entries made therein shall be verified upon the
oath, or in the case of a known quaker, the affirmation of the person by whom those entries shall
have been made, and as often as the said books and papers shall be so returned, other books and
papers shall be furnished upon like demand by the proper officers of inspection, to the said
dealers and distillers respectively. And the said books and papers shall from time to time while in
the possession of the said dealers and distillers, lie open for the inspection of, and upon request shall
be shewn to the proper officers of inspection, under whose survey the said dealers and distillers
shall respectively be, who may take such minutes, memorandums, or transcripts therefrom as they
may think fit. And if any such dealer or distiller shall neglect or refuse to keep such book or
books, paper or papers, or to make such entries therein, or to shew the same upon request to the
proper officer of inspection, or not return the same according to the directions of this act, he or she
shall forfeit for every such refusal or neglect, the sum of one hundred dollars.

And as a compensation to the said dealers for their aid in the execution of this act.

XL. Be it further enacted, That for every quantity of the said spirits not exceeding one hundred and twenty gallons, which shall be sold by any such dealer, in one day, to one person or copartnership, in the casks or cases in which the same shall have been imported, after the said last day
of   next, or delivered out of any distillery (in respect to which the duty hereby
imposed is rated by the gallon) and distilled after the said day, and of the bringing of which into
his or her entered store house, building or other place, he or she shall have given due notice according to the directions of this act, to the proper officer of inspection, and for which he or she
shall have produced to the said officer the proper certificates corresponding therewith, the said dealer shall be entitled to an allowance of one cent per gallon, which allowance shall be estimated by
the inspector of the revenue of each district, according to the evidence of the entries in the books
and papers kept and returned according to the next preceding section of this act, confirmed as to
the production of the proper certificates, by the certificate of the officer to whom they shall have
been produced, and shall also be paid by such inspector, according to such rules as shall be prescribed in that behalf, by the Secretary of the Treasury, which said inspector shall be furnished with
money for such payment out of the product of the duties imposed by this act. Provided always,

---

*The first part of this section seems to be free from any solid objection. It will be constantly the inter-
est of importers (except with a view to smuggling) to bring spirits in large casks. But the object of the
latter part will not be without difficulty. It is however, submitted. Perhaps, if the restriction to casks
of one hundred gallons, should appear improper, it may be limited to a less size, yet such an one as will be
less apt to elude the vigilance of the officers, than the smaller dimensions now in use. The restriction
would certainly add materially to the security of the revenue.*

That if more than one delivery shall be entered as made to one person or copartnership the same shall be deemed but one delivery and one quantity.

XLI And be it further enacted, That the several kinds of proof herein before mentioned marking the casks, vessels and cases containing any distilled spirits shall be in the order in which they are mentioned by the words—"First Proof—Second Proof—Third Proof—Fourth Proof—Fifth Proof—Sixth Proof —" ... And that it be the duty of the Secretary of the Treasury to prescribe ... ficers of Inspection and of the Customs, ...

And to the end that wanton and oppressive seizures ... owners and importers of ...

XLII Be it further enacted, That in any prosecution or action ... any Inspector or other officer of Inspection for ... such Inspector or Officer to justify himself by testimony ... making the said seizure upon which, and proceeding ... every such action or prosecution, or in any action ... such collector or other officer, for the ... trial shall be by jury. And in any action for ... spector, the jury shall nevertheless ... to the true amount in value thereof which ... spirits seized, in consequence of such seizure ... six per cent per annum, on the value ... time to the time of restoration ... provided that no damages shall be ... office or certificates or by reason of any ... the spirits in any entered house, or other ...

XLIII And be it further ... such prosecution or action ... his office, he shall be sued or ... certain office, until the judge who ... verdict

XLIV And be it further enacted, that ... granted pursuant to his ...

XLV And be it further enacted, that ... shall neglect to perform any of the ... the intent and meaning of this act ... age, such person or persons shall, ... spector or other officers, ...

To the judgment nevertheless, that ... unknowingly erred in the execution ... and sufficient amends to the party aggrieved ...

XLVI Be it further enacted, That ... other person acting in aid of the ... against him or them to tender ... agent or attorney, and in case ... any action which may be brought against ... any other plea or pleas with leave ... upon issue joined thereon the ... they shall give a verdict for the ... that or plaintiffs shall become nonsuit ... be given for the defendant or defendants ... be intitled to, and shall recover costs ... no, or insufficient amends were ... tiffs and such damages ...

XLVII And be it further enacted, ... or persons for any thing ... within three month next ... which the cause of action ... suit may plead the general issue ... evidence. And if a verdict ... become nonsuited, or discontinue ... against such plaintiff or plaintiffs ... shall have costs awarded to him, her or them, ...

L

And in order that persons who may have incurred any of the penalties of this act without wilful negligence or inattention of fraud, may be relieved from such penalties,

XLVIII. Be it further enacted, *That it shall be lawful for the judge of the district court, of the district within which such penalty or forfeiture shall have been incurred, upon petition of the party who shall have incurred the same to inquire in a summary manner into the circumstances of the case, first causing reasonable notice to be given to the person or persons claiming such penalty or forfeiture, and to the Attorney-General of such district, to the end that each may have an opportunity of shewing cause against the mitigation or remission thereof, and if upon such enquiry it shall appear to the said judge that such penalty, or forfeiture was incurred without wilful negligence, or any design or intention of fraud, it shall be lawful for him to remit the same, and to cause any spirits which may have been seized, to be restored to the proprietor or proprietors upon such terms and conditions as shall appear to him reasonable. And the decision of the judge, if the terms and conditions prescribed by him be complied with, shall be conclusive on the parties. Provided, that such penalty, or the value of the spirits forfeited, does not exceed two hundred dollars. But if the amount of such penalty or forfeiture exceed five hundred dollars, the person or persons claiming the same, may, within three days after such decision shall be pronounced, appeal therefrom to the Supreme court of the United States, which court shall summarily hear the parties, and either confirm or reverse the decision of the district judge, as shall appear to them proper. Provided always, That prior to the last day of May, in the year one thousand seven hundred and ninety, such fine shall in no case exceed one half the penalty or one half the spirits forfeited, or the value ...

XLIX. And be it further enacted, That all penalties and forfeitures to be incurred by this act, shall be for the benefit of the person or persons who shall make a seizure, or who shall first discover the matter or thing whereby the same shall have been incurred, ... the inspector of the revenue shall give information thereof to such inspector or ... thereout for the United States the amount of the duties payable on the spirits, in which such penalty or forfeiture may have been incurred. And such penalty, and forfeiture shall be recoverable with costs of suit by action of debt, in the name of the person or persons entitled thereto, or by information in the name of the United States of America. And it shall be the duty of the Attorney-General of the district wherein any such penalty or forfeiture may have been incurred, upon application to him, to cause suit to be instituted for such ... Provided always, that no officer or inspector, other than the officer or officers who ... be entitled to the benefit of any forfeiture unless notice of such seizure by him made, ... having been given within twelve hours next after such seizure to the said chief officer or officers. ... such case the United States shall have the entire benefit of such forfeiture.

L. And be it further enacted, That if any person or persons shall counterfeit, or forge, or cause to be counterfeited or forged any of the certificates herein before directed to be given, or shall knowingly or wilingly accept or receive any false or untrue certificate of the tenor of the same, or shall fraudulently alter or erase any such certificate after the same shall be given, or knowingly or wilingly publish or make use of such certificate so counterfeited, forged, false, untrue, altered or erased, every person or persons so offending, shall for each and every offence, severally, forfeit and pay the sum of one thousand dollars.

LI. And be it further enacted, That any person or persons that shall be convicted of wilfully taking a false oath or affirmation, in any of the cases in which oaths and affirmations are required to be taken by virtue of this act, shall be liable to the pains and penalties to which persons are liable for wilful and corrupt perjury.

LII. And be it further enacted, That if any person or persons shall give or offer to give any bribe, recompence or reward whatsoever, to any judge or inspector of the revenue, in order to corrupt, persuade or prevail upon such officer, either to do any act or acts contrary to his duty in the execution of this act, or to neglect or omit to do any act or thing which he ought to do in execution of this act, or to connive at, or to conceal any fraud or frauds relating to the duties hereby imposed on any of the said spirits, or not to discover the same, every such person or persons shall for such offence, whether the same offer or proposal be accepted or not, forfeit and pay the sum of one thousand dollars.

LIII. And be it further enacted, That if any person or persons shall assault, resist, oppose, molest, obstruct or hinder any inspector in the execution of this act, or of any of the powers or authorities hereby vested in him, or shall forcibly rescue or cause to be rescued any of the said spirits, after the same shall have been seized by any such inspector or officer, or shall attempt or endeavor so to

---

* A discretionary power to remit or mitigate penalties in laws of this nature is indispensible. It is peculiarly so in the commencement. Heavy penalties are frequently incurred through inadvertence, misconstruction or want of information. Instances of this kind have happened under the existing system. The discretion however which is proposed to be given in the outset, is to be abridged at the expiration of a period which will allow sufficient time for persons to become acquainted with the law.

do, all and every person and persons so offending, shall for every such offence, for which no other penalty is particularly provided by this act, forfeit and pay the sum of five hundred dollars

LIV And be it further enacted, That if any such inspector or officer, shall enter into any collusion with any person or persons for violating or evading any of the provisions of this act, or the duties hereby imposed, or shall fraudulently concur in the delivery of any of the said spirits, out of any house, building or place, wherein the same are deposited without payment, or security for the payment of the duties thereupon, or shall falsely or fraudulently mark any cask, case or vessel, contrary to any of the said provisions, such inspector or officer shall for every such offence forfeit the sum of one thousand dollars, and upon conviction of any of the said offences, shall forfeit his office and shall be disqualified for holding any other office under the United States

LV And be it further enacted, that it shall be lawful for the Inspectors of the revenue, and when required by any such dealer, they are hereby required to provide blank certificates, in such form as shall be directed by the Secretary of the Treasury, and in the case in which certificates are hereby directed to be issued or granted by the said dealers, to furnish them therewith the blanks in which certificates shall be filled up by such dealers, according to the nature and truth of each particular case, subject to the penalty heretofore declared for granting or using false or untrue certificates. And every such dealer shall from time to time, when thereunto required, account with such Inspectors respectively, for the number of certificates received by him, and for the disposition of such of them as shall have been disposed of, and shall produce and then true certificates thereto to the said Inspector, and shall pay for every certificate for which he cannot truly clearly account, the sum of fifty cents

LVI And be it further enacted, that in every case in which an oath or affirmation is required by virtue of this act, it shall be lawful for the Inspector of the revenue, or any of them, or their deputies, or the ... deputy of one of them where ... in retainment in district, to administer and take their oath or affirmation. And ... wherever there are more than one Inspector in a district, any one of them may execute all and any of the powers and authorities hereby given to the Inspectors of the revenue. Provided, that it shall not be admitted to take any oath, affirmation in any case in which according to the nature of the appointment or service, and the true intent of this act, the authority is or ought to be several

And for the encouragement of the export trade of the United States

LVII Be it further enacted, that in any of the said spirits whereupon any of the duties imposed by this act shall have been paid or secured to be paid shall after the laid out ... ... be exported ... the United States to any foreign port or place, there shall be allowed and paid upon such export ... thereof, by way of drawback, equal to the duties thereupon, ... excepting on the ... spirits ... this act imported, deducting therefrom one cent per gallon ... ... the allowance ... specified within the United States ... ... such spirits exported, two cents per gallon ... and ... after the duties have accrued ... and of ... ... on all spirits ... at any time ... exported into the United States. Provided always, that no such allowance shall not be made unless the said exportation shall be verified in all ... ... the regular ... prescribed by this act. And provided further, that nothing herein contained shall be construed to alter the provisions in the said act now ... concerning drawbacks or allowances, in nature thereof, upon ... simple ... to to be ... ...

LVIII And be it further enacted, that in order to entitle the said exporter or exporters to the benefit of the said allowance, he, she or they, shall previous to putting or lading the same on board of ... ... enboard of ... ship or vessel for exportation, give twenty-four hours notice at the least, to the proper officer of inspection of the port from which the said spirits shall be intended to be exported of his, her or their intention to export the same, and of the number of casks and cases ... either of them, containing the said spirit so intended to be exported, and of the respective marks by the act, and of the place or places where the said spirits shall be then deposited, and of the place to where and ship or vessel in which they shall be to intended to be exported. Whereupon it shall be the duty of the said officer to inspect, by himself or deputy, the casks and cases so noticed for exportation, and the quantities, kinds and proofs of the spirits therein, together with the certificates which ought to accompany the same according to the directions of this act, which shall be produced to him for that purpose, and if he shall find that the said casks and cases have the proper marks according to the directions of this act, and that the spirits therein correspond with the said certificates, he shall thereupon brand each cask or case with the word "Exported," and the said spirits shall, after such inspection, be laden on board the same ship or vessel in which notice shall have been given, and in the presence of the same officer who shall have examined the same, and whose duty it shall be to attend for that purpose. And after the said spirits shall be laden on board such ship or vessel, the certificates aforesaid shall be delivered to the said officer who shall certify to the Collector of the said port the amount and particulars of the spirits so exported, and shall also deliver the said certificates which shall have been by him received to the said collector, which shall be a voucher to him, for payment of the said allowance.

Provided nevertheless, and be it further enacted, That the said allowance shall not be made, unless the said exporter or exporters shall make oath, or if a known Quaker, affirmation, that the said spirits so noticed for exportation, and laden on board such ship or vessel, are truly intended to be exported to the place whereof notice shall have been given, and are not intended to be relanded within the United States, and that he or she doth verily believe that the duties thereupon charged by his act, have been duly paid, and shall also give bond to the collector, with two sureties, one of whom shall be the master or other person having the command or charge of the ship or vessel in which the said spirits shall be intended to be exported; the other, such sufficient person as shall be approved by the said collector, in the full value in the judgment of such collector, of the said spirits to intended to be exported, with condition that the said spirits (the dangers of the seas and casualties excepted) shall be really and truly exported to, and landed in such ports and places without the limits of the United States, according to the late treaty of peace with Great-Britain as shall be specified in such bond, and that the said spirits shall not be unshipped from on board of the said export vessel, whereupon the same shall have been laden for exportation, within the said limits, or at any ports or places of the United States, or relanded in any other part of the same (shipwreck or other unavoidable accident excepted)

Provided also, and it is hereby enacted, that the said allowance shall not be paid until six months after the said spirits shall have been so exported

IX. And be it further enacted, that if any of the said spirits after the same shall have been entered for exportation, shall be used for any purpose whatever, either within the limits of any state of the United States, or within four leagues of the coast thereof, or shall be relanded within the United States, from on board the ship or vessel wherein the same shall have been laden for exportation, (unless in cases of necessity or distress to save the ship and goods from perishing, which shall be immediately made known to the principal officer of the customs residing at the port nearest to which such distress or vessel shall be at the time such necessity or distress shall arise) then not only the spirits so shipped together with the casks and cases containing the same, but also the ship or vessel in or on board which the same shall have been so shipped or laden, together with her gun, furniture, ammunition, tackle and apparel, and also the ship, vessel or boat into which the said spirits shall be unshipped or put, after the unshipping thereof, together with her guns, furniture, ammunition, tackle and apparel, shall be forfeited, and may be seized by any officer of the customs, or of inspection

X. And be it further enacted, that the said allowance shall not be made when the said spirits shall be exported in any other than a ship or vessel of the burthen of   tons and upwards, to be ascertained to the satisfaction of the collector of the port from which the same shall be intended to be exported

XI. And be it further enacted, that the bonds to be given as aforesaid, shall and may be discharged by producing within nine years from the respective dates thereof (if the delivery of the spirits in respect to which the same shall have been given, be at any place where a consul or other agent of the United States resides) a certificate of such consul or agent, and if there be no such consular agent, then a certificate of any two known and reputable American merchants residing at the said place, and if there be not two such merchants residing at the said place, then a certificate of any other two reputable merchants, testifying the delivery of the said spirits, at the said place, which certificate shall in each case be confirmed by the oath or affirmation of the master and mate or other like officer of the vessel in which the said spirits shall have been exported, and when such certificate shall be from any other than a consul or agent, or merchants of the United States, it shall be a part of the said oath or affirmation, that there were not upon diligent enquiry to be found two merchants of the United States at the said place Provided always, that in the case of death, the oath or affirmation of the party dying, shall not be deemed necessary And provided further, that the said oath or affirmation, taken before the chief civil magistrate of the place of the said delivery, and certified under his hand seal, shall be of the same validity as if taken before a person qualified to administer oaths within the United States or such bonds shall and may be discharged upon proof that the spirits so exported, were taken by enemies or perished in the sea, or destroyed by fire, the examination and proof of the same being left to the judgment of the collector of the customs, naval officer, and chief officer of inspection, or any two of them, of the place from which such spirits shall have been exported

XII. And be it further enacted, That the prosecution for all fines, penalties and forfeitures incurred by force of this act, and for all duties payable in virtue thereof, and which shall not be duly paid, shall and may be had before any justice of the peace or court of any state of competent jurisdiction, or court of the United States, of or within the state or district, in which the cause of action shall arise, with an appeal as in other cases · Provided, that where the cause of action shall exceed in value fifty dollars, the same shall not be cognisable before a justice of the peace only

XIII. And be it further enacted, That this act shall commence and take effect as to all matters therein contained, in respect to which no special commencement is hereby provided (except as to the appointment of officers and regulation of the districts) from and immediately after the last day of   next.

(S C H E D U L E K.)

ESTIMATE of the probable product of the funds propofed for funding the debt and providing for the current fervice of the United States, including the prefent duties on imports and tonnage.

	Dollars,
Probable product of the duties on imports and tonnage, according to the acts of the laft feffion, - -	1,800,000

Including the State of North-Carolina, this eftimate may be faid to correfpond with the ftatement made by the committee of ways and means during the laft feffion, which ftatement the Secretary is inclined to think is as near the truth as can be now obtained.

In the preceding eftimate are comprehended wines, diftilled fpirits, teas, and coffee, amounting to about - -	600,000
Which being deducted, leaves - - -	1,200,000
From which deducting 5 per cent for expence of collection, -	60,000

Leaves nett product, - 1,140,000

Probable product of duties propofed.

Imported.

1,000,000 gallons wine, at - - 20 cents, -	200,000
4,000,000 gallons diftilled fpirits, at - 20 - -	800,000
700,000 pounds bohea tea, at - 12 - -	84,000
800,000 pounds fouchong and other black teas, at 20 - -	160,000
100,000 pounds green tea, average at - 25 - -	25,000
1,600,000 pounds coffee, at - 5 - -	80,000

Made in the United States.

3,500,000 gallons diftilled fpirits from foreign materials, at 11 cents,	385,000
3,000,000 ditto, diftilled from materials of the United States, at 9 cents,	270,000
	2,004,000
Deduct for drawbacks, and expence of collection, 15 per cent.	300,600 1,703,00

Dollars, 2,843,400

Lightning Source UK Ltd.
Milton Keynes UK
UKHW03f0412220818
327578UK00005B/581/P